Transforming
Thornhill Lees

the story of a village transformed by industry

Contents

Transforming Thornhill Lees
Published 2013 by Kirklees Council

All text is the copyright of the
authors, except where stated

Designed and typeset by
Andrassy Media
www.andrassymedia.co.uk

ISBN number 978-0-9576832-0-4

Font cover image:
Maurice Greenbank in his
Thornhill Lees allotment
© Amanda Crowther

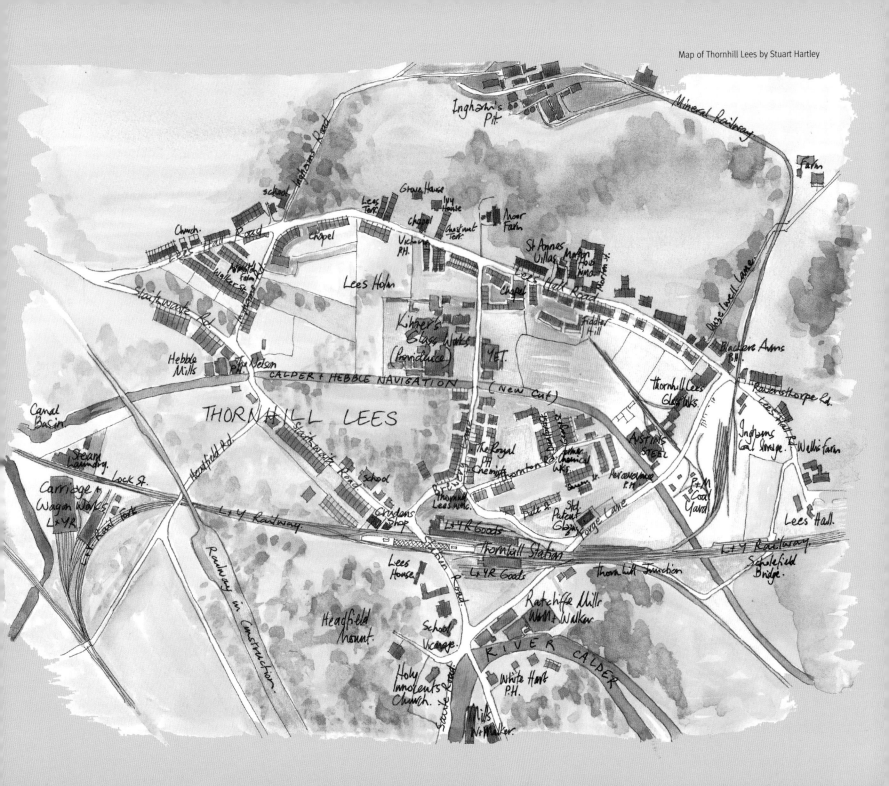

Map of Thornhill Lees by Stuart Hartley

Introduction

'**I'm in my 80s now. My first job was at Ingham's Colliery when I was 14 and I've had many jobs since. I never went out of the village and I never had a day's unemployment!**' *Maurice, 2009*

'Industry created Thornhill Lees. Transformed from rural farm land to a hive of industry, there was a time when smoke from countless chimneys almost blotted out the sky. It gave us a wealth of employment that lasted for a great many years. The economic security it brought created a wonderful community whose families can easily be traced back several generations.' *Nigel*

'If you walk or drive around Thornhill Lees today, you will see houses built in different periods. You will notice a few shops, two schools and land waiting to be developed. It might seem a rather sleepy place, but it wasn't always like this. A hundred years ago, the industries born as a result of the industrial revolution in Thornhill Lees were noisy, lively and thriving, supported by the benefits of the canal and the railway. Most of the workers lived in Thornhill Lees and walked to work. Women did a daily shop, using village stores rather than those in Dewsbury. Milk and coal were delivered to homes and the post man would go round twice a day. A plethora of pubs, clubs, churches and chapels provided people with opportunities to pray, play and celebrate together.

'Sadly, the workplaces that bound the people of the village together are nearly all gone and hence the shops and the community they served. Another transformation is taking place; the village has become a dormitory village for people who work much further afield. Most of the residents who remember the days of industry have died or moved on. A new community of families live here with next to no knowledge of its history. Now is the time to record that history and consider what the future holds.' *Ann*

'This book will tell you something about the businesses and the people who made them great. Residents and former employees of its factories, mills and businesses have contributed their knowledge, family histories and personal memories to tell the story of a village transformed. History is revealed through the words and pictures of its people. Local school children have made contributions too.' *Trevor*

'Hopefully, we are providing future generations with a picture of Thornhill Lees as it was. A lot happened in a short space of time. It was always a place where people came to try things out, work hard and take risks. Maybe, today's children can learn from that.' *Norma*

'It might seem completely different today but if you look closely, you will find visual clues and the past will come to life. We cannot put sounds into a book so you will need your imagination for those. Read the book, take a walk, use your eyes, and imagine the wheels and cogs turning, the whistles blowing, the steam hissing, the clogs rattling, and the people groaning, yawning, singing and laughing.' *Ann*

Thornhill Lees Exhibition Group
Kirklees Community Heritage & Education Team

Opposite: Aerial view of Yorkshire Electric Tranformers works, Thornhill Lees, 1960s

Charlotte Kilner

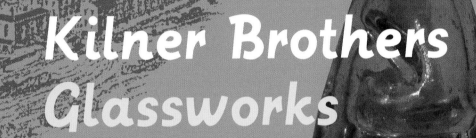

Kilner Brothers
Glassworks

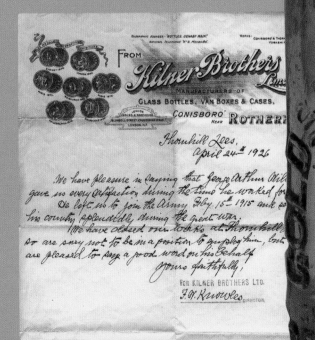

FROM
Kilner Brothers Ltd
MANUFACTURERS OF
GLASS BOTTLES, VAN BOXES & CASES.
CONISBORO' NEAR ROTHERH

Thornhill Lees,
April 24th 1926

We have pleasure in saying that George Arthur Will
gave us every satisfaction during the time he worked for
He left us to join the Army Feby 15th 1915 and se
his country splendidly during the great War.
We have closed our works at Thornhill
so are sorry not to be in a position to employ him, but
are pleased to say a good word on his behalf
Yours faithfully,
FOR KILNER BROTHERS LTD.
J.W. Knowles DIRECTOR.

Kilner Brothers Glassworks

The Kilner Dynasty

John Kilner set up his glass bottle works in Thornhill Lees in 1844 on premises belonging to the Ingham family and tried to make his company independent of rail and steamship by having boats built to take the bottles direct to the Thames Wharf in London.

The canal was used for sand and limestone delivery to the works. John Kilner was the travelling salesman while his sons looked after the manufacturing processes. Father and all three sons had experience of bottle making.

In 1850 Kilner's eldest son Caleb went to London and established a warehouse in Brick Lane from which the bottles were distributed around London. In 1869 they moved to much larger premises near King's Cross Station.

Initially the works was producing around 20,000 bottles a week but improvements in technology, especially the opening of the first of Siemens gas furnaces in 1873, led to much greater productivity. By the 1890s it had the capacity for 300,000 bottles a week plus glass stoppers and other items.

By this time 600 people were employed, some of which lived in the 56 cottages built next to the works by Kilner Bros. By 1894 the Providence Works covered some 11 acres and was lit throughout by electricity. The chimneys of the Providence Works dominated the landscape and three quarters of the village population were employed by Kilners. John Kilner's sons and grandsons watched the glass empire grow.

John Kilner, founder

Smoke in the Glass

"No man has the right to interfere with the supply of clean air"
Judge in 1870

In 1870 the Kilners found themselves fighting a lawsuit brought by neighbouring landowner Lord Savile who objected to the volumes of smoke issuing from the furnace chimneys. Farmers claimed the crops were being poisoned by the smoke and dust. In 1871 the firm was given three months to buy and install new furnaces. George and William Kilner pulled down three of the offending furnaces and installed up-to-date Siemens gas models, which cut down emissions and the consumption of fuel.

Kilner Bros and their workforce were also involved in regular disputes on the subject

of wages and working conditions. There were frequent lock outs.

However, conditions and trade continued to improve. Kilners won prizes and awards and developed the famous "Kilner Jar", a screw topped, rubber sealed jar for preserving fruits and other produce. Local bottle blowers developed a reputation for being skilled in the production of every kind of bottle whereas their European counterparts stuck to blowing one class of bottle. Another factory opened in Conisborough in the 1860s to cope with the demand for bottles.

The glassworks in Thornhill Lees closed down in the 1920s. By then it needed a lot of money spent on it to buy new equipment and keep up with competitors but there was nobody in the family left to take it on, none of them were interested. They only cared about spending money which they all did.
The firm went bankrupt in 1937, the Conisborough site closed and the United Glass Bottle Company took the design rights for Kilner jars.
Margaret M

Paperweights and marbles

My dad worked at Kilners as a bottle blower when he was younger. He left when the factory closed and then worked at Wormalds and Walker. This must have been before 1923. My dad made this paperweight. It's what they did at the end of the shift with the left over glass – made things to take home. It was always tucked away in the cupboard, kept safe until someone used it as a doorstop!
George

I remember playing on Kilner's tip. You had to be careful, as there were still bits of glass about. All us kids played there. We found these sort of prisms from fancy lamps people would have, like chandeliers. They were like kaleidoscopes.
Dorothy

One of my hobbies when I was a little kid was to climb in the old works and find bottles with glass marbles in the necks. There were hundreds and thousands of them. We broke the glass to get the marbles out. Then we'd sit on the curb edge for ages rubbing the

marbles to get them smooth and round because when they first came out, they had little blobs on.
Keith

My mother had a memory of going to the bottle works as a child in about 1918 and watching her father blow glass. I'm not sure when I became aware of the family history because of course, the factory closed long before I was born. By the time I wanted to find out more in the 1980s it was almost too late, even then.
Ann

Kilner Brothers Glassworks
And there's more...

Dear Readers

Kilner's Glassworks — the Bottles are all the colours of the rainbow. One of the bottles had a marble in it when you put water in the bottle the marble moved. The little jolly jars of jam were in little bottles. Heavy horse's for pulling the crates. Hand made bricks for the kilns of Kilners.. best wishes from Hafsah Masood.

Kilner's Glassworkers
Thornhill Lees
Dewsbury
England

Glass from the last firing at Kilners

"People brought some treasures from Thornhill Lees to show us at school. Ann showed us lots of beautiful old bottles and jars made at Kilner's glass factory. Afterwards we made some postcards and showed them to our families at Thornhill Lees Library. Here are more interesting facts about the Kilner family and the people that worked there..."
Year 3 pupil at Headfield School

Margaret's father and cousins

In addition to the glass bottle making departments, Providence Works contained large warehouses and workshops for the manufacture of boxes and crates for mineral and beer bottles, packing rooms and suites of offices.

Kilner's produced bottles for mineral waters, confectionary, jams, jellies, marmalades, drugs, oils, pickles, fruit, sauces, perfumes, wines, spirits and beer. The London warehouse held an immense stock of between five and six thousand different varieties of bottles and jars of all shapes and sizes.

Kilner's sales representatives, known as "travellers," went to America, Australia, New Zealand, India and Africa.

Mary-Ann Kilner lived in St Ann's Villa on Lees Hall Road....
'**It was old, big and cold. I remember the bathroom, it was huge and the toilet was set in mahogany all covered in painted flowers but there was no heat. I don't know how my Great Grandma stood it in there when she had her daily wash!**'
Margaret M

Kilner's developed 'infant feeders'...
"These feeding bottles are a small world of invention in themselves, and the utmost care is applied to arrange them that they should be perfectly adapted to convey warm milk and prepared foods and yet be safe in use and easily kept clean."
Kilner's 50 Years brochure

Mary-Ann Kilner, driving her mother Charlotte

Colours of bottles were carefully chosen according to the intended contents of the bottles. The strongest bottles containing mineral waters were of a greenish tint which were richer in silica than in lime. Bottles containing English beers were black, chosen to "exclude rays of light detrimental to the process of maturing." Green, black, amber and blue were all colours used to control the effects of light upon medicines, wines, beers and even poison.

Mary-Ann Kilner's father – George Kilner – was a prominent member of the Thornhill Local Board and fought long and hard for gas and water supplies to be available in the village. In the late 1800s, drinking supplies had to be fetched from pumps and water for washing purposes had to be collected from the canal. Mary-Ann's mother Charlotte Kilner brought a modern wonder to Thornhill Lees when she purchased the first washing machine!

Mr George Knowles married Elizabeth Kilner (daughter of George) in the 1860s and began to work for the family firm. He eventually became one of the firm's directors. He was at the works ready to start work at 6am every

Kilner's workers, late 1800s

morning and quite accustomed to touring the works at night to see that all was well. In 1921, during the last year or so of the firm's existence, when there was no necessity for his constant attendance there, he visited almost as regularly as he had done in previous years. The Knowles family were residents of Thornhill Lees for many generations from the early 1700s onwards and lived at Ivy House.

'Kilner's built a number of cottages in the village. Mary-Ann had 15 built on Kimberley Street alone and then there were Kilner's Cottages – they are gone now. There were more on Lees Hall Road and Fiddler Hill. They had the money to build and they had their own brick works. I was sent round them all to collect the rent. I was only a young girl then.'
Margaret M

Telegraphic Address:- "BOTTLES, DENABY MAIN."
National Telephone "N.º 9. Mexboro̊".
Works:- Conisboro̊ & Thornhill Lees, Yorkshire.

PRIZE MEDALS INTERNATIONAL EXHIBITIONS.
SYDNEY 1879. LONDON 1862.
PARIS 1875. MELBOURNE 1888-9. PARIS 1878.
PHILADELPHIA 1876. MELBOURNE 1880.
LONDON OFFICES & WAREHOUSE. BLUNDELL STREET. CALEDONIAN ROAD LONDON, N.7.

From *Kilner Brothers Limited,*

MANUFACTURERS OF

GLASS BOTTLES, VAN BOXES & CASES,

CONISBORO' NEAR ROTHERHAM.

Thornhill Lees,
April 24th 1926

We have pleasure in saying that George Arthur Wilby
gave every satisfaction during the time he worked for us.
He left us to join the Army Feby. 15th 1915 and served
in splendidly during the great war.
As we have closed our works at Thornhill Lees
are not to be in a position to employ him, but we
to say a good word on his behalf

Yours faithfully,

FOR KILNER BROTHERS LTD.

F. W. Knowles DIRECTOR.

The last Kilner chimney comes down

"It was said that when the glassworks finally closed and the furnaces cooled, the overall temperature in Thornhill Lees fell noticeably."

Helen

The works closed in 1922 but it wasn't until1937 that the last Kilner chimney came down. It was 132 feet high and was difficult to demolish because it was so well built in 1893. Large groups of local people gathered to watch it come down. Children at the school begged to be able to stand on chairs to watch the process through the classroom windows. The workmen had to dig right underneath the 14 square feet base to prepare it for the fall. The chimney contained 50,000 bricks which subsequently became the property of Brooke Bros who owned the land.

My father worked at Kilner's as a young man, first as a gatherer, then as a glass blower from 1883 to 1902.
I well remember as a school boy sitting on the canal bank opposite the works watching the barges being unloaded of their coal and timber.
Ron

My great grandfather Alfred Dobson was a crate maker there and my father Reuben worked there too. My mother, at the age of 8 used to take the breakfasts for the men at 8.30am and then the dinners at 12.30 in two baskets. These were for two neighbours and she watched the bottles being made. She never found out how they put the marbles in!
Thelma

My father, Tom Long, was a groomsman for Kilner Bros. When they sold the horses, Mr J.R. Kilner got a motor car and being a very smart man, my Dad asked if he would like him to be chauffeur, which he did. Mr Kilner lived at Morton House and liked to go to Bridlington very much in the car.
Frank

Kilner horse and dray, with the works in the background

Baby peaceful in his cot—
Everybody wonders what
It is that makes him sleep so tight,
Never waking all the night.

Bless the little cherubim,
DORMY blankets cradle him !

DORMY

Rex Honey,
piecener, 1950s

contd.

D/Weaving
B/Willeying
B/Scribbling
Surveyors
R/Finishing
B/Scribbling
D/Weaving
D/Willeying
D/Scribbling
R/Scribbling
B/Willeying
B/Willeying
B/Willeying
B/Scribbling
B/Scribbling
D/Scribbling
D/Scribbling
B/Twist. Hank.
B/Scribbling
B/Willeying
Warehouse
R/Scribbling
R/Scribbling

D/Weaving
D/Weaving
B/Willeying
B/Scribbling
Surveyors
Canteen

Norma Robinson
Ethel Quayle
Georg Topalu
John Hazlegrave
Czeslaw Stefaniak
Mary Walshaw
David Irvine
Ryszard Klicki
Michael Smyth
Florence Hinchcliffe
Jack Watson
Vincent Lenczinski
Doreen Thompson
Mary Rennick
Doreen Taylor

Parkinson
Robert K. Alfred

Elizabeth F. Byram
Rex Waite
John Thompson
Gordon Duncan
F. Hemingway
Frank Grundell
Marjorie Auty
Cynthia Blackett
C. Haines

D/Weaving
B/Twist. Hank.
B/Scribbling
Surveyors
B/Twist. Hank.
B/Feeder
B/Willeying

B/Twisk. Hank.
B/Frame Spinning
D/Tier-on
Dyeing
Whipping
R/Scribbling
D/Tier-on
B/Twist. Hank.
B/Frame Spinning
B/Willeying

Wormalds & Walker

Every evening, the mill's "10 o'clock gun" would be fired to show all was well. The bang or explosion could be heard all over the district. It became a kind of benchmark for timekeeping. Young people would be told to be "home by the Gun."

Rex

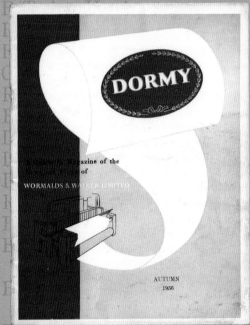

DORMY

magazine of the
of
WORMALDS & WALKER LIMITED

AUTUMN
1956

Wormalds & Walker

From fulling to blanket production

Thomas Cook was an expert salesman. He was responsible for selling blankets to America. Wormalds & Walker's international trade began with him.
Stanley Oldroyd

As early as the 14th century a fulling mill existed at the end of Fall Lane. With a ford providing access across the river, it soon became the hamlet of Dewsbury Mills.

By 1797, John Hague and Thomas Cook were manufacturing broadcloth and blankets. All weaving and spinning took place outside the mill in weaver's cottages.

In 1811 John Hague junior of Crow Nest married May Wormald from Gomersal, whose brother invested heavily in the mill. In 1820 the mill was lit by artificial light from its own gas works and harnessing water power from the River Calder. By 1846 a weaving shed had been added, although some weaving was still done outside. In 1902 the last hand loom weaver died.

Chinese wedding blanket

By 1866, considerable trade was being done with America, South America and Africa as well as a flourishing trade in this country. By 1878 partners John Wormald and John Walker gave the mill the name that many residents of the village remember. The production of blankets and associated products by Wormalds & Walker was highly successful for the next 100 years, attracting the attention of celebrities and royalty both in this country and abroad.

Continental quilts were the death of blankets. The works kept up with the latest developments but finally gave in gracefully and closed in 1986.
Jeffrey

"I remember when I went to W & W for my first interview and they asked me 'Have you got any other family members here?' It helped if you already had links with the firm."

Sheila

A family firm

My grandfather Joseph Lynn was a blanket raiser in the early 1900s. After the wool was scoured it went on to a machine to raise the nap on the blanket. My father was a blanket fuller. He worked at the mill right up to his death. My dad received a certificate for 50 years service and I got a certificate for serving a 6 year apprenticeship.

Jeffrey

There was a lady called Mrs Key who was retiring and the firm suggested she start a club using the hut on the field – 'The Key Club.' Basically, a group of retired workers met there to make rugs and toys. Every year they had a sale. W & W provided a lot of the materials. People felt they were still doing something useful.

Jeffrey

It was a caring firm. If someone was very ill, they'd think nothing of sending them off to convalesce for a couple of weeks. A group of Italian weavers came to work at W & W after the war. Initially, they lived in a hut on the sports field. Not speaking much English, it was a tough time for them. W & W bought Woodleigh, a house just up from the church. They made it into small units for the Italian workforce.

Sheila

DORMY FAMILIES (II)

Families of workers at W & W, featured in *Dormy Magazine*

13

The best in Britain, the best in the world

"We were making blankets for the war effort and special blankets with pictures of spitfires on them."
Mary

Mary with a Spitfire blanket from the 1940s

For over 100 years Wormalds & Walker were producing high quality blankets for this country and particularly abroad. As well as the standard blankets, edged with satin, we produced Chinese wedding blankets and decorative blankets for Canada, America and Basutoland. There were frequent visitors to the mill, the Chieftainess of Basutoland being one memorable visitor.
Sheila

Everybody played their part. My mum was a weaver. My dad delivered blankets, by horse and cart. I remember he used to take me to see the horse in the stables. It was called Dolly and she was lovely. Later on he drove a three wheeler van and then in the 50s a four wheeler van.
Christine

John Wormald, the director was a real mill man. He used to visit every department and speak to all the weavers every morning. Well, there were 1,000 looms so it took him until dinner time to do this! The workforce was valued and the workforce in turn valued the firm and their place in it.
Jeffrey

Often as children we saw the men from Wormalds and Walker wheeling out blankets on barrows, to take them to the tenterfields to hang them out to dry. Even with all that smoke and stuff around belching from the chimneys, they still put the blankets out to dry.
Mary

Mill workers with singer James Baskett for Workers' Playtime

WORKER'S PLAYTIME

ANOTHER packed canteen, a hush as the minute hand creeps to the appointed time, a roar of applause and yet another Workers' Playtime from Dewsbury Mills is "on the air."

Throughout the morning rehearsals had been going on. Engineers wandered about performing mysterious operations ; the piano tinkled incessantly ; odd two-and three-bar snatches of harmony floated from the dressing rooms ; a debonair young man strolled about the stage carolling happily to himself.

On a chair in front of the stage, a pretty and self-possessed girl kept glancing at a stop-watch, gazing dreamily into space and announcing, "Ten seconds too long," and one or other of the artists would break into

incomprehensible conference. And all the while, aloof and unperturbed, the producer, seemingly disinterested but in reality observing every small point.

Dead on time the show began. First the Meritones, a slick and tuneful group of vocalists who were specially formed for the recent Festival of Music in Venice. Then Jack Watson, tall and jovial, comedian and impressionist son of the late Nosmo King, a famous comedian.

Following Jack Watson came the moment all the teen-age girls had waited for. To squeals of delight, on came Denis Lotis, one of the most popular singers in the country. South African born Denis had recently been tested for a film lead opposite glamorous Lana Turner, but unfortunately for him,

page twelve

In 1957 'Workers' Playtime' was broadcast from the Dewsbury Mills canteen, as reported in *Dormy magazine*

High jinks in the canteen

It wasn't only the work you went to Wormalds & Walker for, it was the social life. You paid a shilling a week out of your wages towards the sports club. Stanley Oldroyd organised all of that. There was a bowling green, cricket, tennis, badminton, a junior rugby team and a ladies' football team. Two people were employed just to look after the bowling green and cricket field! And then there was the operatic club – the Wormald Players.

We had a big canteen with a fairly big stage. The big names that appeared at Dewsbury Empire all seemed to come to Wormalds & Walker. Mill tours for celebrities were a regular thing and they all got a blanket to take away with them. Even James Baskett (Uncle Remus in Disney's *Song of the South*) visited. And of course, the BBC's *Workers' Playtime* was broadcast from the mill on a number of occasions.

They say marriages are made in heaven. Ours was made at Wormalds & Walker.

We met at a staff dinner that was held at Dewsbury Town Hall. Jeffrey offered to take me home and that's how it started. When we got married, we got a pair of blankets.

We still have them – a bit worn now but still good.

Sheila and Jeffrey

"I can remember the Christmas parties – oh they were brilliant. There were plenty of kids, loads of us. There were clowns and food and a present at the end from Santa."

Christine

15

Below: Jeffrey Cooper Lynn's apprenticeship certificate, 1952

Right: Jeffrey's father's 50 years service certificate, 1962

This Certificate is issued by the Directors of

Wormalds & Walker
Limited
DEWSBURY · YORKSHIRE

to _Joe Lynn_

in recognition of their appreciation of the completion of

_50_ years

able service with the company their hope for a continuation of appy association for many years.

In token of which the common f the company was hereonto l in the presence of the Directors

day _2nd March, 1962._

Wormalds and Walker
Limited
DEWSBURY MILLS, RATCLIFFE & BRITANNIA MILLS,
DEWSBURY · YORKSHIRE

This is to Certify that

Jeffrey Cooper Lynn

has successfully completed his term of apprenticeship of 6 years at the _Dewsbury_ mills of the company, and is entitled to recognition as a skilled _Stockwright_

Commenced _18th April, 1946_
Terminated _18th July, 1952_

Particulars of work on which employed _Wood and Iron Working, Fitting and Joinering, General engineering including Turning, Slotting and Shaping_

In witness whereof the Company has caused its Common Seal to be hereunto affixed.

The Common Seal of Wormalds and Walker Limited was hereunto affixed in the presence of

P. J. Walker Director
John Wormald Director
J. A. Elliott Secretary

Dated this day _22nd June, 1953._

The first woman to swim the channel

Eileen Fenton, the first woman to swim across the channel in 1950 was born and brought up in Thornhill Lees. In 1951, she visited Wormalds & Walker to increase her knowledge of industrial history in her role as a teacher rather than a swimmer. But as you can imagine, she was still a celebrity and it was still very special to have her at the works.

Sheila

Right: Eileen Fenton's "instructional visits" to Wormalds and Walker, as reported in Dormy Magazine

Celebrated Visitors . . . .

Miss Fenton, who was the first woman across the channel in the "Daily Mail" Cross-channel swim in 1950 and only narrowly failed in the same race in 1951, is now teaching at Earlsheaton Junior School. In order to increase her knowledge of local industries she made two instructional visits here and we were all very pleased to see her.

Harry Watson and the
ten o'clock gun

The 10 o'clock gun

Many people in the village remember the 10 o'clock gun which was fired every night by a night watchman as a signal to the mill owners that all was well at the mill, possibly originating from the time of the Luddite riots. The practice of firing the gun, originally a blunderbuss, continued for about 150 years, even throughout World War II when the Ministry of Defence was persuaded to let the tradition continue. The gun could be heard for a radius of up to five miles and many people set their clocks by it.

Young adults and teenagers would be told to be 'home by the Gun.'

Harry Watson, Night Watchman, fired the gun during the 1940s. Harry was born in 1890 and worked in Combs Pit from the age of 16 years. He left mining because of ill health and joined Wormalds and Walker in 1941. It was reported in a national newspaper that he was the guardian of a 'Dewsbury Institution.'

Rex

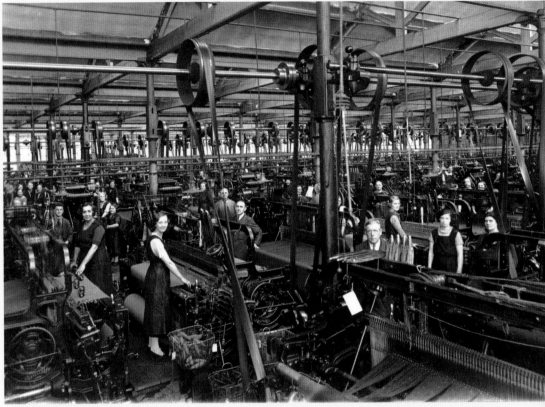

Above: Weaving shed at W & W, 1930s

It's ten o'clock
The Gun's gone off
I cannot stay no longer
For if I do my Mum will say
You've been wi' lads up yonder.

17

Wormalds & Walker
And there's more...

"Sheila worked at Wormalds & Walker for a long time. She showed us the blankets that they made and told us stories. One day everyone from the mill went on a big train to London for a festival. Here are more stories..."

Dear Reader

Dewsbury is a place of blanket mills and Mines.
A long time ago people made blankets.
After War they needed people to work in the mills. people Like my Grandfather came to Thornhill lees to find Work.
They lived in Small houses.
It was hard to learn + understand English. They missed their family.
After a while they called their family over. Now we live and work here and are settled. from
Abigail

Old and New Stories

Thornhill lees past and present

Dewsbury

England.

Mary Lodge, Miss Dormy 1950

In September 1951 Wormalds & Walker took a thousand workers on two specially commissioned trains to the Festival of Britain in London, leaving six watchmen to look after the mill. They took "Matilda" the lamb with them for a 'guess the weight of the lamb' competition. Terry Thomas presented the prize of two blankets to the lucky winners.

For many years, Wormalds and Walker appointed a queen of the mill – 'Miss Dormy.'

In the 1950s, some Thornhill Lees families working at the mill could claim associations with Wormalds & Walker for well over a hundred years.

In 1952 the DORMY brand was launched by Wormalds & Walker. To the roar of the 10 o'clock gun, 1250 balloons soared skywards in celebration.

"In these days of rush and bustle we are all too inclined to decry the past and those who lived in it. We here at Wormalds & Walker should have only praise for those giants of former days, those ancestors of yours and mine who built this firm on such sound foundations. Wormalds & Walker did not earn for itself the name of The Rock for nothing."
William Wormald, 1952

At one time the firm owned 64 acres of farmland in Thornhill Lees.
Making blankets was a seasonal trade. So when orders were down in the summer months, people were taken out of the works and set to work on the land, until the orders came in again.
Stanley O

At the end of the war, Wormalds had a big bonfire of celebration with fireworks. I remember a girl there who was an evacuee and when the fireworks started to go off she was absolutely terrified because she associated the noise with the sound of bombing and gunfire.
Norma

Accidents did happen. Auntie Winnie worked at Wormalds and Walker. She was a weaver and she was pulling off some wool, but it was a manmade yarn, and she wrapped it round her finger to pull it off. It wouldn't give and it took her finger off. Then her arm went into the machine. She lost her finger and her arm was damaged but she went back to work. She couldn't weave again and so she went into the pattern room.
Helen

Festival of Britain Train
commissioned by W & W

"Wormalds & Walker always welcomed foreign workers. My dad went to work at the mill after he arrived here in the 60s. He was a weaver and that's where he worked for a year or so before my mum came over from India."
Fatima

Pearson and Moody were the local hauliers of coal from the pits to the local industries like Wormalds & Walker. Uncle Leonard was a wagon driver for Pearson and Moody. In the school holidays, he used to let me go with him collecting coal from the coal yard which was on Brewery Lane and delivering it to all the local mills that had boilers.

Stanley H

Wormalds & Walker always welcomed foreign workers. My dad went to work at the mill after he arrived here in the 60s. He was a weaver and that's where he worked for a year or so before my mum came over from India.

My dad was quite educated but he had to take what he could get and do all the unsocial hours. So I remember him doing nights at Wormalds & Walker. I thought it was funny that he'd just gone to sleep when I went to school, but you don't really concern yourself with those things when you're a child – where the money's coming from and who puts food on the table as long as it's there.

Fatima

The Poles were exceptionally good and hard working people.

Stanley O

My family originally came from a little village called Keralgam in Gujerat, India. My dad first came to England in 1955 to find work. After the war my uncle was the first to come here and he found a lot of work here. So my dad followed him over and that's how the rest of the family arrived. He worked at the Dormy blanket mill and worked very long hours. He arrived in England with this suit and wore it whenever he wasn't working, and his shoes were always polished.

Kateja

Kateja's dad arrived in England in the late 50s, and started work at W & W

19

Coal queens

The Thornhill Collieries

Joshua Ingham III

"When Ingham's Colliery was operating, it was permanently light."
Roy

Background image:
'Timber Lads' by local artist
Malcolm East

The Ingham Collieries

Miners at Combs, 1915

Mining the Mountain

Ingham's Colliery was a dark, dirty place, that really was going back in the dark ages as far as collieries were concerned. The washing plant was like something you'd imagine seeing in Oliver Twist.
Roy

After Savile Estate, the main landowners in the Thornhill area were the Ingham family. Coal was mined for local use from the 17th century. By 1780 Joshua and Benjamin Ingham, once cloth merchants, were sending fine quality coal as far as London using the Calder Navigation. By 1851 Joshua Ingham the Third employed 100 colliers, 100 boys, 35 pit hill labourers, 13 artisans and 10 female pickers.

The Inghams, whose family home was at Blake Hall in Mirfield, also had considerable influence as farmers and local dignitaries, owning a fulling mill at Lockwood, and a cotton mill near Halifax. Under the control of Edward Ingham the mining interests were consolidated into two major collieries: Combs Pit and Inghams Pit, employing men from the top and bottom of the Mountain.

Having made use of the River Calder and later the canal for transporting coal, a purpose built railway was finally built, linked to the main line . The company's first locomotive was purchased in 1876.

In 1893 the company was badly hit when there was a major explosion at Combs Pit in which 139 miners died. The Inghams retained a presence on the board until nationalisation in 1947 and the collieries survived until 1972.

Pat's dad, known as 'Mad Jack'

Mad Jack and Steam engines

My father Jack Sykes worked at Ingham's Pit as a winder all his life. The men were literally in his hands.

The cage doors would be closed and then he would start pulling the levers and the dial would tell him how fast they were going down. Some of the men used to call him "Mad Jack" because he let them go down faster than he should have done.

When he worked week-ends, mum put dad's dinner in a basin with a saucer on top and rice pudding in a jam jar. It was my job to walk along the fields to the engine room where dad would be waiting. I would sit there while dad ate his dinner and then he'd walk along to the lamp room and watch me go down. The pit selected Coal Queens and one year my sister was Coal Queen.
Pat

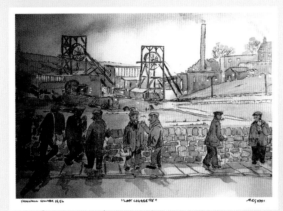

I went to work at Ingham's Colliery as an apprentice electrician. The pit was very poorly lit and winding the coal out of the mine was done by steam engines. I can't remember the engines at Ingham's Colliery ever being modernised. I moved to Combs Colliery. There was a tunnel linking the two, and the coal was sent from Combs to Ingham's to be processed.

Some of the coal from the Colliery went down to the coking plant, and they extracted Benzol which is virtually petrol. The coke ovens site was a fearsome place with its flames and hissing steam. It was quite something.
Roy

When I was little I slept at the front of the house on Lees Hall Road and I clearly remember lying in bed listening to the miners walking along the road in their clogs. They'd turn left at the side of St Anne's House and walk alongside the allotments up to the coke ovens. When I was about 13, a family moved in next door. The daughter who was a bit older than me said "Oh look, there's a big fire up there!" It was the coke ovens she was so alarmed about.
Ann

HY. WHITEHEAD,   FRIEND SENIOR,   WILLIE LIGHTOWLER,
SQUIRE SHIRES,   JOHN GARFITT,   RICHARD WOOD,   J. MALLINSON.

Two villages mourn

I have worked at the pit for thirty years and have never known any gas before. It was thought to be free of it.
Richard Wood, survivor

On 4th July 1893, a gas explosion at Combs Pit killed 139 local men and boys. Crowds rushed to the scene anxious for news of the entombed miners. Most had died as a result of the fire or the deadly effect of the gas. Colliers at Ings Pit, Thornhill Lees made their escape when noxious fumes issued from the outlet that formed a means of communication between the two pits.

Houses in both villages drew their curtains. Coffins made at Ingham's works were filled and carried to their respective homes. Dewsbury cancelled its programme of festivities for 6th July to celebrate the marriage of the Duke of York to Princess Mary because 'anything feastal would be out of place.'

Only seven men survived the explosion, having spent over 30 hours entombed. Later they were taken to the seaside to help them recuperate. A picture of them hung in Combs Colliery until the closure in 1975.

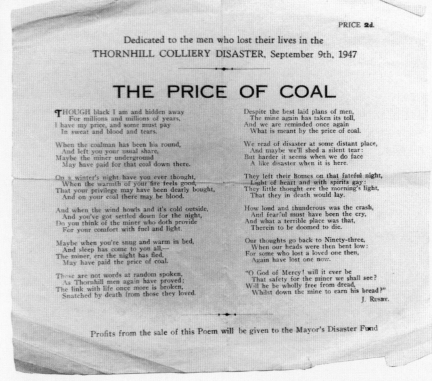

PRICE 2d.

Dedicated to the men who lost their lives in the
THORNHILL COLLIERY DISASTER, September 9th, 1947

THE PRICE OF COAL

THOUGH black I am and hidden away
　For millions and millions of years,
I have my price, and some must pay
　In sweat and blood and tears.

When the coalman has been his round,
　And left you your usual share,
Maybe the miner underground
　May have paid for that coal down there.

On a winter's night have you ever thought,
　When the warmth of your fire feels good,
That your privilege may have been dearly bought,
　And on your coal there may be blood.

And when the wind howls and it's cold outside,
　And you've got settled down for the night,
Do you think of the miner who doth provide
　For your comfort with fuel and light.

Maybe when you're snug and warm in bed,
　And sleep has come to you all,—
The miner, ere the night has fled,
　May have paid the price of coal.

These are not words at random spoken,
　As Thornhill men again have proved;
The link with life once more is broken,
　Snatched by death from those they loved.

Despite the best laid plans of men,
　The mine again has taken its toll,
And we are reminded once again
　What is meant by the price of coal.

We read of disaster at some distant place,
　And maybe we'll shed a silent tear:
But harder it seems when we do face
　A like disaster when it is here.

They left their homes on that fateful night,
　Light of heart and with spirits gay:
They little thought ere the morning's light,
　That they in death would lay.

How loud and thunderous was the crash,
　And fearful must have been the cry,
And what a terrible place was that,
　Therein to be doomed to die.

Our thoughts go back to Ninety-three,
　When our heads were then bent low:
For some who lost a loved one then,
　Again have lost one now.

"O God of Mercy! will it ever be
　That safety for the miner we shall see?
Will he be wholly free from dread,
　Whilst down the mine to earn his bread?"
　　　　　　　　　　　　　J. RUSBY.

Profits from the sale of this Poem will be given to the Mayor's Disaster Fund

More danger

Ella Clarke's dad Jesse was the sole survivor of the second pit explosion, this time at Ingham's pit in 1947. He was found hanging over a rope with a broken back. Afterwards, he could strip down his motorbike, but his wife had to set things out for him to put it together, because the trauma affected his memory. I think there were 12 men killed – it was the last major accident at the pit.
Roy

When explosion happened, I was worried because George used to go to the shaft early every morning to examine it, making sure water wasn't running down into the pit chamber. Explosion was early hours of morning. Had he gone down?!
Mary

It was funny, there were no lights at pit that morning. As we were going along road a neighbour shouted 'You'll not be going down this morning George, there's been an explosion.'
George

The Ingham Collieries
And there's more...

"Maurice the miner loaned some of his treasures to us to show at school for the day. The pick axe was so, so heavy! It was dangerous in the mines and even children like us worked there. Did you know that Ann Bronte looked after Mr Ingham's children?"

Dear Reader

The mine in thornhill Lees was dirty and dangerous. Miners blasted and dug the earth to get the coal. They had lamps to see heavy pick axes. Coal was burnt on fires in houses and factories to keep people warm. canaries tested for the gas. The mine manager making money.

Best Wishes
Sufyaan Ali

The Mine
Thornhill Lees
Dewsbury
England

The Ingham family first claimed local interests in coalmining in 1736 and still had an Ingham on the company's board in1947 when the coal industry was nationalised.

In 1810 Joshua Ingham became the owner of the Thornhill Lees Ironworks on Forge Lane. The forge for rolling and working iron was subsequently let to James Day and William Coe, followed by Shaw & Taylor under the name of Thornhill Lees Iron Company. Eventually the Inghams sold the works to William Firth who immediately promoted a new company *The Thornhill Iron & Steel Company Ltd*. The company thrived for many years, finally selling its site to Austins in 1927.

There was a terrible boiler flue explosion at Thornhill Lees Forge in August 1914 which claimed 8 lives and badly injured 30 men. The explosion was so loud it could be heard all over Thornhill Lees and workmen at the forge

were thrown in all directions. Managing director Mr Wheeler escaped injury, only because he turned back to collect his fountain pen that morning and was slightly late to work. The injured men were badly scalded and suffered serious lacerations. The explosion caused such a stir in the community that postcards were printed in memory of six of the men who died. Sadly, there were no existing photographs of the other two men.

In 1851 Joshua Ingham III was charged with manslaughter after a four year old boy wandered onto the unattended railway at Cromwell Colliery and was killed by wagons carrying coal. He was found not guilty and continued to serve as a magistrate.

In 1840 The Manchester and Leeds Railway paid the sum of £700 to the Ingham estate in compensation for land taken for the new railway.

In 1858 Joshua Ingham paid the Navigation £100 to cross the Thornhill Cut and connect his new colliery at Combs to the main line. They were initially reluctant to lose the monopoly over the carriage of Ingham coals. A railway bridge at Thornhill Lees to serve Ings pits was not agreed upon until 1878.

Ingham's Collieries supplied coal to the Kilner glassworks until the firm's closure in the 1920s.

In 1839 Anne Bronte became a governess to the Ingham family at Blake Hall, Mirfield at the age of nineteen. The Ingham children were not accustomed to having to abide by any rules and persistently disobeyed, teased and tormented Miss Bronte. She was not given permission to inflict any forms of discipline and and failed miserably to teach them anything. On leaving for her Christmas holidays, she was told her services would no

Above: Miners' Gala
by Malcolm East

Right: Blake Hall,
Mirfield, home of
the Inghams when
Anne Bronte was
the children's
governess

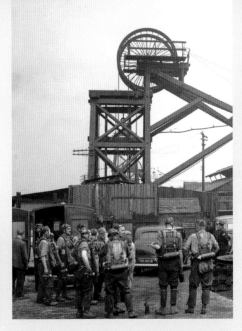

The rescue team at Ingham's
mine in 1947

longer be required. The whole episode was so traumatic for Anne, she reproduced it in almost perfect detail in her novel, Agnes Grey, where Blake Hall became 'Wellwood House' and the Inghams were depicted under the guise of 'the Bloomfield family'. Mary Ingham, while giving no support to Anne in the controlling and disciplining of her children, was said to be very kind to her.

John Shaw worked as an apprentice for Tom Green the butcher. I think he's 90 some now. It was part of his job to go to the bottom of what we call Pit Lane where the miners walked to and from the pit. He'd go up there on his push bike with pork pies in his basket and wait for the miners to come down. When he served them the pies, he'd proddle a hole in each pie and pour in gravy from an enamel jug with a lid.
Keith A

Thornhill Lees was a wonderful, adventurous place to grow up in. We used to go sledging down the old pit stacks in winter. They'd be covered in snow and you'd have a chilly ride down but then you could end up in the stream which was warm and steaming like a hot spring because the stacks were burning inside. Now health and safety laws wouldn't allow it, it would be fenced off.
Nigel

I got my calling up papers in 1944. I went to Huddersfield for me medical and Leeds for the actual navy interview. I'd been working at the pit from being a nipper at 14. At the end of September, I was due to join HMS Pembroke, Chatham but Mr Brinsdon, the foreman blacksmith at pit said "They're not having you, I want you, they're not having you!" And that was it. They somehow convinced the navy I was

needed at the pit. I was young and I was eager so I was a bit disappointed. But after time I realised I was better off where I was. I finished off joining the Home Guard to show willing. I was on fire watch at the pit at night.
George

A childhood memory of the colliery was looking towards the pit shaft to look for the flag. If the weekly output record had been broken, they flew the Union Jack from the top of the pit head.
Bill

My grandfather worked at Combs pit and my Granddad was chosen for the mine rescue team, connected to a national rescue team. He knew what to do in a crisis and seemed to have the aptitude for it.

There was a disaster at the pit in the 40s, and my granddad spent two days underground trying to rescue miners that were trapped. There'd been a big explosion and a fire and of course, fatalities.

He was given a certificate for his rescue work but the family threw it away. They didn't realise it might be important. When people did heroic things it wasn't talked about much. They brag about things now and write books or go on television. But in those days accidents in the pits were two a penny.
Trevor

James Austin & Sons

Iron and Steelworks

"For almost 150 years the name of James Austin &
Sons was famous. Its products spanned the world and
its endeavours helped make Britain great."
Nigel

Facing page: Unloading a barge at Austin's

James Austin & Sons
Iron and Steelworks

Early beginnings

"For almost 150 years the name of James Austin & Sons was famous. Its products spanned the world and its endeavours helped make Britain great."
Nigel

When James Austin arrived in Dewsbury in the 1840s he worked as a millwright for Harrison and Pagett. Pagett eventually retired and Austin entered into partnership with Harrison, changing the business from that of millwrights to the stocking of iron products. Iron for factories, mills, wagons; carriages and blacksmith's materials were the chief line of business. In 1864, James Austin added saw blades for the cutting of stone, marble and granite. Originally made of iron, by 1893 they were replaced by carbon steel blades.

James' son Harry engaged an office boy named Joseph William Wilson who went on to become managing director of the firm after the deaths of James and Harry. In 1904 the 23 year old Wilson, who was promoted from office boy to salesman, steadily built up a network of contacts regionally and

The Forge bought by Austin's, Thornhill Lees

nationally. The greater bulk of Austin's business depended on him, especially during WW I when the firm was placed on the Admiralty supply list.

In 1927 the site of the old Thornhill Iron and Steel Works was advertised for sale and Austin's bought it. The site was completely cleared and two large bays were built for the fabricating and stocking of iron and steel. Railway wagons ran into the new works to unload materials. By 1935 Austin's obtained their first contracts for structural steelwork. The future looked promising.

DEATH OF THE FOUNDER

JAMES AUSTIN

comparatively quick succession, three figures were now to leave the scenes new so well and in which they had laboured so hard.

first of these was the founder of the business, James Austin, who died on the ctober, 1892, in his seventieth year. For over forty-two years he had developed siness in Dewsbury until at his death it was a sound solid firm, described ocal newspaper at the time as "of large proportions". His wife had died three arlier and when James Austin died he left three sons and three daughters.

second bereavement in the family followed in less than a month. On the ctober, the eldest son, Alfred Rider Austin, died at the age of forty-six. ough his health had been a source of anxiety to his father for many years, Rider Austin was in many respects a remarkable man. Trained by his to be an engineer he possessed many inventive abilities and one of his

> "A tremendous amount of work was carried out for the war effort and a considerable amount was carried out by local women who were specially trained for this type of work."
> Nigel

WAR AGAIN

Nerves of steel

In 1938, as the country geared itself up for the impending conflict, Austin's was already supplying the steelwork for four radar installations on the south coast. Existing buildings of strategic importance were reinforced and camouflaged with products provided by the Thornhill Lees steelworks. The company fabricated steel blast proof doors for heavily reinforced underground control centres.

During 1941 a torpedo storage depot was equipped, a heat treatment plant required for producing tank armour plating was supplied and erected, and the company undertook the bulk production of Bailey bridges.

In 1942, an urgent request was received from the Air Ministry for portable hangars to accommodate repair work in the new aerodromes being prepared for the American Air Force.

The closing years of the war brought more work to Austin's. Many parts of the country began extensive re-building programmes of bomb damaged areas. The need to produce structural steelwork was now greater than ever.

When the firm's family link was finally severed with the death of A Wilson and his sons, the firm was sold to Firths, and subsequently to Truman's in the late 1990s when the works finally closed is doors for good.

Illustrations from Austin's Anniversary booklet, celebrating 100 years of the firm

Portable hangars supplied by Austin's
to support the war effort

In 1942, an urgent request was received from the
Air Ministry for portable hangars to accommodate
repair work in the new aerodromes being
prepared for the American Air Force.

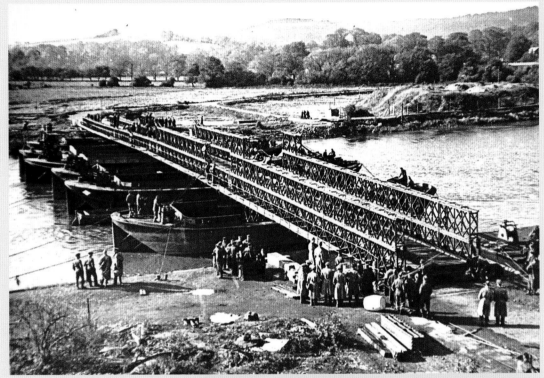

Left: Constructing a Bailey Bridge, a type of portable, pre-fabricated truss bridge developed by Donald Bailey for military use during WWII.

Bleow, from left to right: Austin's loading bay; Fabrication bay; Grimsby Football Stand

33

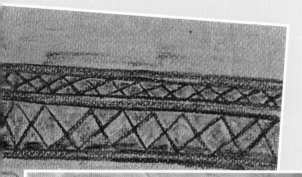

James Austin & Sons
And there's more...

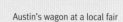
Austin's wagon at a local fair

> "Men made steel in Thornhill Lees and the steel went all over the world. Some of it was sent by barge on the canal. Joan's dad was a bargeman. He had a best hat."

Bowler hat worn by Joan's dad

Harry Austin, son of founder James Austin, took a special pride in the firm's teams of horses that pulled Austin's wagons. They were a familiar sight to the mills and factories of the district. On several occasions they won prizes in the Dewsbury May Day Parade.

During the war, Austin's fitted screens and covers to blast furnaces and coke oven plants so that the plants could operate during the hours of darkness without visible light being admitted to the sky.

My dad, Walter Stenthorpe, worked as a bargee on the Calder and Hebble Navigation in the early 1900s. This was his "best hat". He fought in WWI and was badly wounded. He couldn't go back to being a bargee after that. It was hard work.
Joan

Like everywhere else in Thornhill Lees, Austin's suffered from regular flooding...

It flooded every year – two or three inches we got most times. One year I remember I was on nights. There was a big flood and I rang for the manager because I was in charge of the nightshift. I asked him would he come in and he gave me instructions about everything we could lift up off the floor; all the electrical and welding equipment and everything. We had to get it up onto the workbenches, up onto the top and then I think the next day there was about 3 foot of water.

Oh yes, it used to flood pretty bad. Since they built the flood relief down on Thornhill Road, it's been a lot better. It stopped a lot of flooding, especially around Thornhill Lees.
Keith

Keith receiving his long service award

"We used to make stoves for people on the allotments for heating the greenhouses. In those days, the local firms were still helping the communities they were working amongst."
Keith

There was a big do in 1950 to celebrate 100 years of Austin's success. I was still an apprentice. They hired a train and took the entire workforce to Morecambe: from Austin's, and the two sister companies A J Riley's in Batley and Astley Brooks in Huddersfield. That was a lot of people. They put a meal on and everything for us and gave us spending money.
Keith

Near where the allotments are, there's a pond there that a lot of people don't know about. They used to wash the coal up at the pit and it used to come right round and into there. Every 12 month, the pit people or the Coal Board used to come and dredge it out and it was nothing else but pure coal dust. That's what we used to use at Austin's before we got heating in. We used to build us own stoves and make the coal dust into 'duck eggs.' We'd just put 'em in the stove and leave 'em all night. Next morning you could griddle it out and everything disappeared. It was just dust you were left with.
Keith

Loading trucks

YORKSHIRE ELECTRIC. TRANSFORMER CO. LTD.
DEWSBURY, ENGLAND.

High

"When they were testing the transformers you'd know about it. The noise and the vibration were amazing and quite alarming if you weren't used to it. When the factory closed, the silence was eerie."

Marlene

Front cover illustration from
Yorkshire Electric Transformer
company's brochure, 1950s

Voltage

Yorkshire Electric
Transformer Company

1,000 kVA, 33 kV Transformers at King William's Town, South Africa.

150 kVA Mobile Substation.

150 kVA Underground Transformer.

Yorkshire Electric Transformer Company

The world of transformers

In the 1920s Mr Lydall and Mr Glendenning had the foresight to see that the relatively new power of 'electricity' was going to be one of the wonders of the 20th century and they founded a company in Thornhill Lees called Yorkshire Electric Transformer Company.

The works were built on the site of a former malt house on Brewery Lane and part of the factory was always known as the "malt kiln." Initially the company manufactured small distribution transformers – the ones you see on housing estates – but as time passed, they got larger and sent further afield.

My first recollection of the company was in the 1940s when my parents took me to see my grandparents who lived in one of the cottages alongside the offices. It was in a small wooden hut nearby that my father became the first storekeeper and the first member of my family to be employed there.

The cottages became the first sports and social club before being demolished to make way for the extension to offices and works. On my journey to and from school,

I passed the large entrance to the works where I could see the welding sparks as they fabricated the steel tanks that would contain the workings of the transformers.

Bill

The original offices close to the old malt house

"Transformers were temperamental, quite often they blew up! While testing a transformer, Wilson Oldroyd suffered 50,000 volts passing through him and he lived, even though the surge of power took the top of his head off! Miraculously, he recovered and went back to work."

Stuart

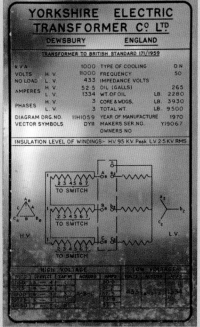

Above: Metal panel screwed to every transformer

Left: A transformer being loaded

"When a transformer left the works by road,
the whole village vibrated."
Pat

Facing page: Ready to roll – a transformer leaves Thornhill Lees

The people who made it tick

That was a great big place, the Transformer, you know. I don't know how many people worked there but it was a big employer in the village.
Pat

As I grew up, the demand for transformers grew and so did the transformers! The extensions to the works to accommodate them were all designed and built in-house. How many firms could do this today? My Uncle Harry, who started there in 1930 as an apprentice coil winder and graduated to being a skilled winder, drew my attention to a vacancy in the drawing office.

I was offered the position of apprentice draughtsman, helping to produce prints for the shop floor.

Being an apprentice, I was given other duties too, the most important of which was going down to Garside's butcher's shop in the morning to buy pork pies for the office staff for their morning break. These were placed on the radiator pipes

to keep warm awaiting Mrs Bentley coming round with cups of tea. The workforce made use of the village shops and amenities and the factory was known as 'The Transformer' by the locals.
Bill

Office staff in the 1960s

Below: A works trip to the Winter Gardens Blackpool, 1945

Right: The new offices in the 1930s

Far right: Demolition during 2009

The success and the social life

I remember we went to the Transformer club for a drink and a game of bingo sometimes. On New Year's Eve, they used to lock the door, so only locals were in there. It was good and there'd be no trouble if you knew everybody.
Christine

In 1965 a whole new assembly shop and testing facilities were built. It was a huge landmark in the village. The crane was capable of lifting 180 tons. The driver,

Donald, who was known by everyone as 'Coco', obviously had a head for heights because the crane track was 60ft above the shop floor.

The directors also decided the company should have training facilities for apprentices, so a training school was built along with a new canteen. This doubled up as a social club and extra social venue for the village. Successful snooker and table tennis teams evolved from the club. When the works closed, some of the ex-employees continued to run it by leasing the premises.

Over the years I progressed to becoming Production Controller. Other young men who became skilled workers were the envy of the world for their workmanship. Transformers were exported to South America, Africa, the Middle East, Turkey and Greece. The firm had manufacturing companies in South Africa and Australia.

YET was more than just another factory. If you got a job there it was a job for life. It was a place where fathers and sons, brothers and sisters and even husbands and wives worked.
Bill

Transferring skills

Unfortunately, companies in the late 60s subscribed to the idea that bigger is always better and YET became part of a consortium. This was the beginning of the end for the company who were eventually taken over by Hawker Siddeley Power Transformers. When things got tough in the 80s, HSPT closed YET in favour of their flagship company in Walthamstow, irrespective of a full order book, worldwide respect for the product, freehold land with room to expand and a conscientious and loyal workforce in Thornhill Lees.

In October 1980, after 21 years of service, I was made redundant and a year later the factory closed. Every cloud has a silver lining because afterwards a colleague and I started our own business and called it Yorkshire Transformer Services Ltd. The name gave us a head start in the business. Within a short time we were leasing a small unit from the property company that purchased the site and we were successful for nearly 15 years, carrying out work for the major power companies operating in the UK.
Bill

Yorkshire Electric Transformer Company
And there's more...

"The fizzing and the buzzing of the big transformers made the village hum. Here are some more memories..."

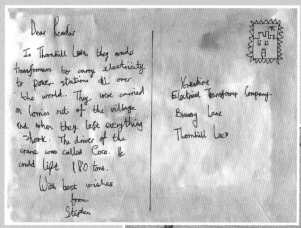

Dear Reader

In Thornhill Lees they made transformers to carry electricity to power stations all over the world. They were carried on lorries out of the village and when they left everything shook. The driver of the crane was called Coco. He could lift 180 tons.

With best wishes from Stephen

Yorkshire Electrical Transformer Company Brewery Lane Thornhill Lees

The largest transformers manufactured at YET weighed 150 tons when completely assembled.

During a fuel crisis YET worked with Rolls Royce to produce generator units for use in the Middle East.

The work force was very proud of the fact that YET held the record for producing transformers in 10 weeks from receipt of the order to despatch of the transformer.

Lesley Driver, the designer of the fabrication shops and testing facilities, also had his own dance band and went on become a director of Dewsbury Rugby League Club.

In the summer, local girls would get on their bicycles in their shorts and ride up and down past the Transformer when the men and lads would be sitting out. You could say the factory transformed lives!
Pat

My husband and I set up an engineering business in 1966 called Chambers Engineering. It began its life in the very large garage attached to Ivy House but we soon moved into part of the old Transformer Factory. I did all the books and learned how to use a capston lathe, centre lathe, drilling machines, a guillotine, and electrical and gas welding and braising. I also went out selling, delivering and talking to customers. We worked for the Transformer Factory too making little flat brass packers cut to a particular shape. On delivery, I always remember the lads saying: 'Thank God it's you lass, it's the only time they all fit when your lad makes them.' This always used to make me feel proud. We ran the business until my husband died in 1997.
Marlene

Family names I associate with YET are: **Baker, Bennett, Broadhead, Chamberlain, Collomosse, Denton, Dunford, Haigh, Holmes, Lockwood, Nicholas, Oldroyd, Peacock, Simpson, Smith, Stokes and Wood, and of course, Beattie.**
Bill

Standard
Patent Glazing

"I can fall out of bed, get on my bicycle, buy my morning paper and be at work ten minutes later and that's brilliant."
Paul

Facing page: Paul with the 1904 pump (named "Kim") which he restored in 2012.

Standard Patent Glazing

No. 6 Section, to carry up to 9' 0"

No. 1 Section, to carry up to 12' 0"

No. 1 Section, to carry up to 7' 0"

Setting the Standard

We're based in Thornhill Lees but we offer a unique product to clients nationwide, including the Royal family.

The company has been around since 1902. Henry Richardson and Frederick Bottomley started a patent glazing company on Boat Sands at the side of the Calder. They moved to Forge Lane, Thornhill Lees, in 1922 and built the factory from scratch. There are machines in the lead shop where we draw lead covers for the glazing bars that have 1904 stamped on them. Those machines are still operating now.

When the company was founded, the recent innovation of lead covered patent glazing bars ensured a positive demand for the product. Patent glazing is a self draining system of dry glazing that does not require maintenance. It does not need external sealing to be water tight. The lead covered bar was the first patent glazing bar. They were all timber at one time. Now we are the only company in the country that makes lead covered bars, particularly for listed buildings. English Heritage, for instance, insist on lead covered bars.

During WWII, the aluminium industry grew rapidly to provide the light metal needed for military aircraft. When the war ended, there was a high demand for aluminium for new building projects. The new technology from this industry was applied to glazing bars and Standard rose to the challenge. We supply skyline, traditional and heritage patent glazing.

Keith G

HENRY RICHARDSON.
1902 – 1951
CHAIRMAN
1910 – 1951

The directors of Standard Patent Glazing, late 1930s

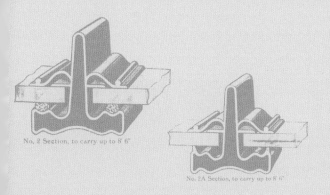

No. 2 Section, to carry up to 8' 6"

No. 2A Section, to carry up to 8' 6"

"There are machines in the lead shop where we draw lead covers for the glazing bars that have 1904 stamped on them. Those machines are still operating now."
Keith G

Working for Crown and Community

In so many places of work you're just a number, whereas at Standard everybody has a name and a face and they're valued.

I started in the drawing office in 1969, and then worked my way up to be contracts manager followed by contracts director. The company has a strong history of employing people from Thornhill Lees. There are quite a few family members working together. There are three brothers who work on the outside installations and one of them works with his son.

The firm has a national reputation but also has its place in the community. One day we would be installing glazing at Buckingham Palace, the next day we could be giving wood to Maurice who had an allotment next door. He had a woodstove and used the wood for that. Basically, if there's anything he wanted, he knew where to come.

The company takes pride in the jobs it does. We did quite a big job at Buckingham Palace a few years ago. They built a new gallery at

the side of the palace and we did all the roof glazing on it. When the IRA blew Manchester up in 1997 we did the work on the Royal Exchange Theatre. We were the only company that could replace its original lead bars.

So much industry has been and gone in this tiny village, like Kilner's glassworks – how could something so huge could just disappear? Standard has weathered the storm and continues to provide a product of quality.

Keith G

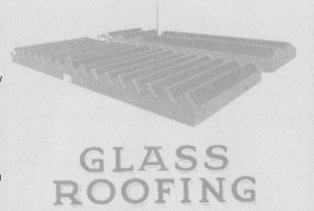

GLASS ROOFING

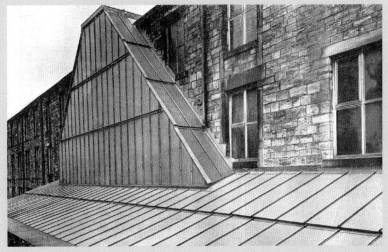

The rope race at Wormalds and Walker, installed by SPG

The roof of the Victoria Quarter, Leeds

Standard Patent Glazing
And there's more...

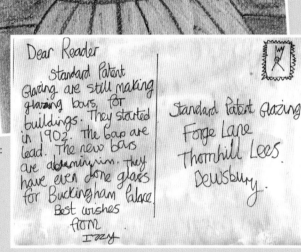

> "Standard Patent Glazing still has a factory in Thornhill Lees after a hundred and ten years. They did the glass for Buckingham Palace and a theatre that had been blown up."

The workshop syndicate won one of Vernon's biggest ever pools payouts in 1973. I think it was about a quarter of a million pounds between about a dozen of them – quite a lot of money then. Everyone went down on a bus to London to receive the money from Vernon's. Morecambe and Wise presented them with the cheque.

When we worked on the Royal Exchange Theatre project, the glass on the job was a unique product too. It was the old theatre glass. The architect found a shard of the original glass and when they cleaned it up, it had a distinctive violet blue colour. That glass was actually replicated by a firm called Solar Glass down in Basingstoke.

Disaster struck as the company prepared to do the Royal Exchange job. The pot for the old lead press blew up. It was the only one in England and the re-glazing had to be done using lead-coated frames. Two engineers picked up the pieces and literally stuck the machine back together using Araldite. Once it was completed, they took it to a Batley foundry where they commissioned a replica.

The job was done and the theatre's domes were restored.

We have done quite a lot of railway stations: Hull, York, Manchester, Darlington, Marylebone, Earl's Court, Paddington, Altrincham, Chester and Harrogate. Manchester Victoria Station involved replacing 864 individual pieces of glass, each one a different size and shape.

We did a job with the Heritage bar again in Cob in Southern Ireland where the Titanic sailed before it hit the iceberg. Basically the ship sailed from Liverpool down to Southern Ireland and then set out on her maiden voyage to America, or its last voyage as it turned out. It was the Titanic Visitor's Centre that we were working on with the Heritage bars.

We had a centenary event at Cedar Court in 2002 and we invited workers old and new and valued clients to attend the celebration. It was very nice to celebrate 100 years of the company. We had the full works – a meal and entertainment. It was all organised from here and it was all very professional and enjoyable. *Keith G*

Dear Reader

Standard Patent Glazing are still making glazing bars, for buildings. They started in 1902. The bars are lead. The new bars are aluminium. They have even done glass for Buckingham Palace.

Best wishes
from
Izzy

Standard Patent Glazing
Forge Lane
Thornhill Lees.
Dewsbury.

Barbara Greenbank with
mushrooms from
Mortimer's Mushroom
Farm at Lees Hall

The entrepreneurs
of Thornhill Lees

"Butchers, bottle makers, bakers and boot makers:
Thornhill Lees had them all. You could shop for most
things without leaving the village."
Helen

October

"Ann came to our school and showed us all the old things her dad used to sell in his hardware shop like the carpet cleaner that worked without any electricity! Here are some interesting stories about more people who had their own businesses..."

Thornhill Lees shops

A diy shop that sold Green shoe polish and pill boxes + ointments Sold bread and buns, pins and tacks and screws Plastic cameras and funny flash bulbs All in the accounts Book.

Best wishes from zaid K

Shops
Thornhill Lees
Dewsbury
England.

A man of hardware and harmony

He was a well known figure. Everybody knew Jack Cruden and his shop.

My grandfather came from Scotland and set up his own business in Thornhill Lees on Slaithwaite Road in 1903. My father, Jack Cruden, continued the business until the 1970s.

He sold small quantities of things but he supplied goods to the bigger companies to such as the Transformer company, and he always stayed open while the workers from Wormalds and Walker came home for their lunch. The siren would go at 12 o'clock signalling dinner time; I'd hear the sound of their clogs and some would pop in to the shop for odds and ends.

It was a treasure trove of scrubbing brushes, pots, pans, stepladders and lots of screws and nails of different sizes. He provided the big companies with ironmongery and the local joiners and undertakers came in for materials they needed to make furniture and coffins.

The goods for the shop came to Thornhill Lees Station and as a child I was sent to collect the goods with a little handcart. I would load this up and bring down the bags of nails and boxes of screws and take them to my father. He was busy but he still had time to be a musician. He played the violin in an orchestra in Dewsbury and the saxophone in a band at the Church Institute. He was always in a rush when going out so I had to put his cufflinks in for him!

Helen

Florence the Shopkeeper

My Great Grandma Florence Ada Wilby ran a tobacconist's shop. From the look of the window, she sold a lot more than tobacco and cigarettes!

Eileen

Devoting 50 years of service to the village

Mr Horsman, the chemist

The shop has always been a part of my life. When it shuts it will be like a chunk of history closing. I've painted the front of that shop, oh it must have been 10 times!

In 1902, an extension was added to an existing house on Brewery Lane and the first chemist shop was opened by John Day.

When I was a teacher, a child brought me some bottles he'd unearthed with the name John Day on them. In 1927 the shop was sold to George Etchells – a typical chemist with a little waxed moustache.

In 1957, my mother and father bought the shop. An additional room to the dispensary was used as a surgery for 3 hours a week and the chemist was in operation until 1972 when Dad died suddenly. My mum Jean took it over as a pharmacy with locums coming in but eventually kept it as a drug store until 2007, providing a much needed service for local people for almost 50 years.

I remember standing in the shop, getting under my Dad's feet in the narrow corridor behind the counter. I used to play with the bottles in the old drawers, enticingly at child level.

We stocked Rich Ruby wine and British Cream Sherry in wooden barrels. People would bring their bottles on Christmas Eve and get them filled up. Fifty years ago each shop had a strict 'division of labour'. You didn't sell things that other shops sold, but of course all that's changed now.

David

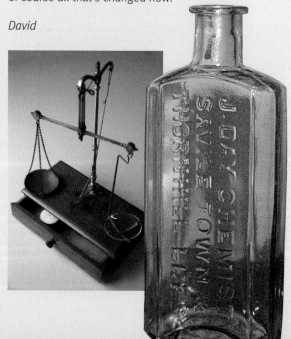

Beatrice the Dressmaker

George the Milkman

My mother Beatrice Bates (nee Goldsbrough), who was born 1911, opened a dress shop in the 1930s at the top of Brewery Lane, where the curiosity shop is now.

This was after having served her time as dressmaker and tailoress in Savile Town and working at *Marshall & Snelgove's* in Leeds and *Brown Muffs* in Bradford.

My granddad was George Blacker and he was the local milkman in Thornhill Lees. I never knew my granddad, he died before I was born.

He had a horse and cart. I guess they used to sell milk out of the jug then, measuring it out in gills. The milk will have come from Broadhead's Farm, near where we lived. When my dad took over he really enjoyed it because he liked meeting people. When the war started and my dad went into the forces my mum had to sell the business but for some time he was a well known figure all over the village and beyond.

Christine

Stanley the Coachman

Stanley Gath founded his bus company in 1956 in Thornhill Lees.

His first bus was an old Bedford which he parked outside his house on Walker Street. Stanley organised day tours to Newquay, Eastbourne and other seaside places. The village supported these trips and Stanley was able to expand his business. Eventually he kept a fleet of buses in a purpose built garage at Lees Hall.

Bill

A Bedford coach used by Stanley Gath

Tom Myers – a man ahead of his time

Above: Tom Myers, Mayor of Dewsbury

Left: Tom Myers' Union Card from his time at Kilner's

My Granddad Tom Myers had a Shoddy and Mungo company called 'Tom Myers & Sons' in a building that was once part of Kilner's Bottle works.

He worked at Kilners as a boy (afternoons only) having already worked at a local mill and mine as a child because the family were very poor. Later on, he endeavoured to catch up on his education at night school and of course he went on to become an MP and later Mayor of Dewsbury.

At the age of 22 he helped to found a branch of the Independent Labour Party in Thornhill Lees. He served on Dewsbury County Borough Council until 1920 when he was elected to Parliament. His success caused a national sensation.

He was a champion of the underprivileged and believed passionately in the principles of co-operation, trade unionism, votes for women and education for all.

At the outbreak of the First World War, he spoke heatedly against Britain's involvement, recommending peace negotiations. In an age when Britain ruled an Empire it took courage to support anti-war policies. Tom was in

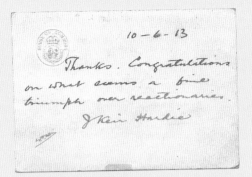

10 – 6 – 13

Thanks. Congratulations on what seems a fine triumph over reactionaries.

J Keir Hardie

constant contact with people such as
Ramsay Mcdonald, Philip Snowden and Keir
Hardie. His wife gave hospitality to Christabel
Pankhurst when she was seeking refuge after
being released from Strangeways Jail. He was
a man ahead of his time.

Jacqueline and Gillian

From
Spen Valley to Westminster

A Spen Lad for Spen Valley !

Printed and Published by H. OGDEN, Cleckheaton, and 35 Unity Street, Bingley.

Top: A postcard from Keir Hardie

Above: By-election flyer, 1920

Left: Tom and Sarah Myers with
Keir Hardie (centre)

The milk of human kindness

Khizar in the late 1970s

Khizar
DAIRY SERVICES
236, HEADFIELD ROAD, SAVILE TOWN, DEWSBURY
W. YORKS. WF12 9JL
Telephone: (01924) 460477

As a milkman, people knew me as a friendly and hopefully an honest person who cared about his community.

I left Pakistan in June 1967 and was brought here as a child. I was a bus driver for some years and then became self employed for at least 12 years operating a milk round on a daily basis. I had a traditional milk float and employed a couple of young runners to work with me.

Gradually, the business expanded. I earned £400 per week at the start. Eventually that went up to £600 per week. I supplied milk to the doorsteps of Savile Town, Thornhill Lees, Ravensthorpe and even as far as Batley Carr.

I was providing groceries as well as milk; fresh veg, bread and general groceries until the arrival of the big superstores threatened it's success. We put up a fight but in the end we couldn't compete.

However, soon after that, I was asked to stand in the local elections. I didn't know what I was getting myself into but I was always interested in local and national politics so I gave it a go and I was elected.

My face was already known from my business. I think I was already known as a person that contributed to the community. My father always said 'How fortunate we are to be in this country. Make the most of it.' He was a great influence on me.

Khizar

Brooke Bros Coal Merchants and Transport Company

Brooke Bros Coal Merchants was established in 1919 by my father and uncle – Arthur and Ernest. They lived in Slaithwaite Road. Originally, they had approximately 15 horses and carts.

They built up the business until they had about 20-30 vehicles. It became motorised in the early 30s with a steam wagon.

Our coal merchants serviced the whole area and the firm was part of the life of Thornhill Lees. We had the field on Slaithwaite Road past the school where you turn up to housing that was at one time garages. We took over Sam Hall's garage which was next to ours.

Thornhill Lees Trinity Rugby League Team

The field coming out to Douglas Street was used for the horses to come out after a day's work. That field, owned by us, was also the field used by Thornhill Lees Trinity Rugby League team.

In 1948 we used the last horse and in 1956 the business became a transport company and a coal merchants. I went into the business with my father and uncle and ran it for quite a few years. In 1963 we sold it to the Hanson Group. I needed a change – to get out and do something else, but there were moments when I did regret that decision.

Brooke Brother removal van, 1950s

59

Edna the Postwoman

During the war, lots of women took on the jobs of the men. I became a postwoman aged 20 and I used to deliver all over this area. I went as far as the top of Ingham Road.

There's a path going up the mountain side and there were a few cottages called 'the back of the Moon' which they pronounced 'back o' moen.' That was the end of my delivery round. I came all the way through Ouzelwell Lane to those farms.

Sometimes I was late back, because I'd gather blackberries. If the inspector asked, I'd say 'I got held up at farms.' He didn't know I had a large jar of blackberries in my jacket.

Once I called at a house on Christmas morning and the man at the door hadn't a stitch on. I said 'You have to sign for this, but I'll turn around whilst you sign.' He said 'Ah ney lass, if you're not bothered, neither am I!' Well, it was a bit much on Christmas morning.

I was chased by a flock of geese up a telegraph pole, charged by a goat and hassled by cows. The goat I remember well and I had to keep pushing it away. The

woman at the house said 'Don't elbow it, it's having a baby.' I said 'Mrs, if it does that again, I'll be having a baby as well.'

We went in to people who were bedridden and we'd make them a cup of tea if they needed it. Did little jobs and such for them. We weren't supposed to but of course we did what was needed.

Edna

'Watkies' the Bakers

Whitsuntide Walk,
Brewery Lane, 1910
(Kirklees Image Archive)

The Watkinson family ran a family grocer's shop on Brewery Lane from the 1930s. In about 1940 they converted the shop into a bakery, baking their own bread on the premises. Initially the baking was done upstairs until they bought the cottage next door, knocked it through and began to bake downstairs. Bread has been baked on the premises ever since.

Malcolm (The Bakery)

The bakery used to make all the teas for Whitsuntide in the 1930s. I was out on Whit Monday at seven in the morning to trim the wagon for the procession and add benches for the Sunday School children and the orchestra. There'd be a procession all round the village and the children would sing hymns. Then we'd come back to the Sunday School room for tea. There'd be two long tables set out. The teas cost 6d a head for adults but was free for the children. There must have been about 30-40 children seated. After tea, on their way out, the children got a "leaving bag" with an apple, an orange, a long bun and a bar of chocolate.

George

An early childhood memory is of my mother taking me to Watkies (Mr Watkinson's shop, now Blackburn's), which although only a few hundred yards from home, seemed to be a long journey. On entering the shop you were immediately struck by the smell of freshly baked bread, the good old fashioned type. Along the right hand side of the shop were stacked tin boxes of biscuits with glass lids. Here you could cast your eyes over the different types: ginger biscuits, cream crackers, morning tea, sports biscuits, all waiting to be weighed out for they did not come in packets then.

To the left were two old fashioned wooden chairs upon which the older members of the village would sit whilst they waited for their turn to be served. I can still picture old Mrs Moses sat there with her long blade skirt nearly touching the floor. Behind the counter would be old Mr Watkinson, always dressed smartly. He was a stalwart member of the Western Chapel opposite where I lived. Alongside him would be Clem Atkinson who did the majority of the serving. Jack Watkinson (son) would be in the back doing the baking, ably assisted by his sister Winnie. On the counter facing you would be stacked

the butter waiting to be cut, patted into shape and weighed, before being carefully wrapped. The sugar would be spooned into a stiff paper bag, weighed and then the top carefully folded over so that the sugar would not spill out. These two items would be weighed on the most beautiful set of scales that you could imagine, a polished brass column supporting the scales. On one side was the pan for placing the immaculately polished brass weights.

Bill

The Bakery in 2009

Lees Old Hall, Thornhill Lees, near Dewsbury.
This old Hall, formerly the residence of the Nettletons, is of great antiquity, dating from the time of the Tudors. In the time of Bluff King Hal it was known as Nettleton's house, and described as such in a deed dated 1634.

Reg the mushroom farmer

One of Dewsbury's oldest buildings – Lees Hall – was brought back to life by mushroom farmer Reg Mortimer in the 1940s. The renovation began with a bet a friend he could renovate it in time for a New Year's Eve party. Reg went on to run a highly successful mushroom farm where many local people found employment.

My mum worked at the mushroom farm planting, weeding and picking for over 20 years. Several members of the family worked there at one time or another. One day she was taken to work on a field off Thornhill Road near Wormalds & Walker but when she got there, the field appeared to be moving. It was full of frogs. She was terrified of them and had to come home!

Barbara

The most significant thing that influenced my life greatly was working at Mortimer's Mushroom Farm at Lees Hall – the hidden treasure of Thornhill Lees. I was a young lad tagging along with my older brother who had already worked there at potato picking time. Reg set me on stoking the boiler of an old traction engine that provided steam for the mushroom growing process. I will always remember that first day looking after that great old engine; I think it must have been then when my love of engineering was born. Reg was very innovative, he was always converting and improving the various machines that were used to make the mushroom compost, creating one machine from parts of another to suit the needs of the farm. He had that "can do" attitude that inspired people. I continued working at the farm at weekends and school holidays. Over the years I learnt by doing, working with the various tradesmen the farm employed, but the best thing I ever learnt was what Reg taught me; believe in yourself and if you put your mind to it, anything is possible.

Nigel

Reg Mortimer, off to collect mushrooms

Nigel's family allotment

My father and grandfather were keen gardeners and had a large allotment garden behind the house. Edric and Harry Ingham grew plants and flowers to sell to local people for many years. At the beginning of the year they grew bedding plants. They made their own compost made up of elements such as leaf mould from the wood behind Crow Royd Farm and silt dug from the river banks after the winter floods.

The greenhouses had a marvellous heating system making use of local waste materials that cost little or nothing at all in their stoves; coke that had spilled off the overloaded wagons from the coke ovens or coal waste from *Pearson & Moody's* coal merchants on Forge Lane. Another fuel favoured by local gardeners was 'Devil's muck' or solidified coal slurry which was in great abundance just over the garden fence! The bedding plants were always ready for the spring bank holiday for people to plant in their gardens. When these were sold, Harry and Edric concentrated on growing a variety of flowers to be cut for and collected by customers or delivered to their doors.

Nigel

Left: Harry Ingham and grandson

Below: Edric's flower garden

Maurice the teacher

Above: Maurice with his dog

Right: Children from Headfield School in Maurice's allotment, 1980s.

I've had my allotment for 58 years. When I worked at Headfield School as caretaker in the 80s, I started a scheme teaching children about gardening. From about Easter, weather permitting, I took two classes per week to the allotment until October. Now the children, some of them had never seen some of the things I showed them, especially the Asian children.

They were all interested, well mannered and worked hard. They helped look after the poultry and worked in the garden area. They planted broad beans and collected eggs. They had a plot of land to do their best with growing seeds and at potato lifting time, they picked all they could. It was learning through doing and it was fun.

We'd 14 classrooms in school and every Monday morning each teacher had a vase of flowers on their desk, all of which the children had grown. The vegetables, when they were ready, were taken home. There were often trails of pea pods on the footpaths because they ate them on the way home.

One class took their vegetables back to school and with the help of kitchen staff they invited me and Mr Ibbot the Head to lunch, to have soup that they'd made, with a roll.

Another class, by way of saying thank you to their teachers, gave them half a dozen fresh eggs each. Children picked them up, packed them and gave them as gifts.

Another time, they took some eggs back to school and the next day I took an incubator into the classroom. They put eggs in incubator and waited. They were thrilled to bits to see the eggs hatch.

I meet these children now, all grown up, out shopping or whatever. They have children of their own now. I can't possibly remember all of them, but they remember me and always say hello. I have a lot of nice memories of my work.

Maurice

Sadly, Maurice Greenbank died in December 2012 while this book was being edited.

Henry Glassby the Bootmaker

Henry and his family lived on Walker Street. Successive generations contributed significantly to the working, religious and social life of the village.

Henry's son, Alfred Glassby, worked for Samuel Firths Ltd for 58 years, beginning as a bookkeeper and eventually becoming a director of the firm. He married Edith Dixon who was a teacher at Lees Moor School.

Alfred was the first secretary of the Church Institute when it opened and Edith was involved with welfare work for men and women serving in the forces as supervisor of the Thornhill Lees Church Rest Centre.

Alfred and Edith's wedding day in 1903
Photo courtesy of Susan Day and Glassby Family History website

Henry Glassby in front of his boot maker's workshop in Thornhill Lees, 1905
Photo courtesy of Susan Day and Glassby Family History website

Life in the village

Entertainment at the Working Men's Club

The club was a constant hive of activity for men, women and children.

When I was a small boy, men from the different local working men's clubs used to dress up in costume and play comic instruments. Thornhill Lees had a very good comic band. They'd turn ordinary objects such as watering cans and scrap items into musical instruments. Some of them had Tommy Talkers attached – they call them kazoos now. The costumes and instruments were intricate and they entertained all the children at the carnivals and galas but they were eager to win and competition was serious. They'd parade round the village and end up on Brooke Brothers' Field on Slaithwaite Road where carnivals were held.

George

As children, we used to go on Thornhill Lees Working Men's Club trips and it was really good fun. We'd get an envelope with some spending money in and tea and drinks when we got there and it always seemed to be to Cleethorpes. We always had a little card each in case we got lost. It said where you'd to be picked up. There were plenty of stewards looking after us all, one to so many children.

Margaret J

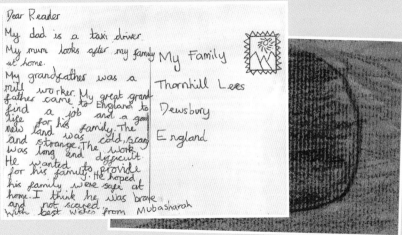

Dear Reader
My dad is a taxi driver
My mum looks after my family at home.
My grandfather was a mill worker. My great grand father came to England to find a job and a good life for his family. The new land was cold, scary and strange. The work was long and difficult. He wanted to provide for his family. He hoped his family were safer at home. I think he was brave and not scared.
with best wishes from Mubasharah

My Family

Thornhill Lees

Dewsbury

England

We went on the club trip from Thornhill Lees Station, always on a Saturday and there were 12 carriages. Coming home very late, the train was too long for the platform and we had great difficulty getting out of the carriages in the dark, then walking home to Walker Street. This seemed like a great adventure at the time.

Stuart

I remember going to dances at Thornhill Lees Club upstairs. It was a dance night on a Friday but you didn't have alcohol. Downstairs was your Thornhill Lees Working Men's Club but then we used to go upstairs to dance. There was an MC and you used to dance and then they'd come on with this water container and we'd have cups of tea and biscuits. No booze obviously because we were all quite young and that was fine because we just wanted to have a good dance.

Margaret J

Coronation party, 1953

Wartime memories

Children celebrating the end of WWII

Norma in her uncle's garden

We were very fortunate in that my Aunt and Uncle kept livestock – pigs, rabbits, hens and ducks. Uncle would go around the village collecting potato peelings and kitchen waste which was used to feed the pigs.

He also took the horse and cart to Dewsbury on market days and collected discarded greens from the stalls. These were then boiled up and pig meal added and fed to the pigs. Come Christmas a pig was sent to the slaughterhouse. Half came back to us and half went to the Government. A local butcher, Mr. Leach, cut our half up into joints and ham and bacon was salted and hung up in the cellar. There was also lots of lard rendered down from the fat.

We had rabbit pies and Auntie dried the rabbit skins and made mittens with them. Everything was utilised.

There were lots of impromptu parties especially at Christmas time when the pigs had been killed and there was plenty to eat. A lot of extended family came and also some soldiers that were stationed nearby. Everyone had a party piece, a song or

Receipt for the teas at the Working Men's Club

Facing page: The women of Thornhill Lees celebrating the end of the war

recitation. It was great fun listening and watching the adults acting the fool.

When the sirens sounded we had to get out of bed, get dressed and either went to the air raid shelter which was dark, cold and damp, or we sat under the kitchen table. There was a Cobbler's Shop on Station Road and I remember taking some shoes for repair when the sirens went off and the cobbler told me to run home as fast as I could. I was very frightened. A bomb fell on Savile Town - houses were destroyed and I think one person was killed. As far as I know this was the only time we were bombed. We were very lucky.

The war in Europe was over and there was great celebration. We had a street party and a large bonfire. The women even went chumping with us. I'll never forget Mrs Smith, a small dumpy lady, who helped us roll a large tree stump that we had found. She huffed and puffed and her face was as red as a beetroot but without her help the kids wouldn't have triumphed.

Norma

The role of the Churches and Chapels

Many of the churches in Thornhill Lees came into being because of the industrial revolution taking place in the village and the financial support offered by mill, mine and factory owners. Working families attended services, processions, family occasions, social gatherings and performances. Special and lasting friendships were formed and skills utilised for the good of all.

Bill

Holy Innocents' Church was consecrated on 23rd June 1858. It owes its existence to the generosity of the Wormald family and Thomas and John Hague Cook of Dewsbury Mills. Joshua Ingham of Ingham Colliery also donated over £3000 to pay for the land and conveyancing costs. The church contains many beautiful stained glass windows, many of which were gifts from the Wormald family. The south window in the chancel was the gift of John Hague of Crow Nest, Dewsbury. Workmen from Dewsbury Mills installed the two bells and the clock.

Sheila

The Church Institute held dances in the large downstairs room. Victor Steel was the M.C. Slow, slow, quick, quick, slow. The highlight of the week for the younger people were the film shows with Mr Robinson working the projector – *Old Mother Riley, Charlie Chaplin, Laurel and Hardy* and best of all cowboys and Indians. There was always much cheering and whistling.

Norma

My father was very involved at the Independent Chapel, which is where the Kingdom Hall is now. There was always something going on, all sorts of activities. I've got a photo of my Dad playing in a production of *Robin Hood* (above). He's on the second row up from the bottom, second from the left. He played Little John.

Dorothy

My great grandfather, James Taylor, was the first trustee and caretaker at the Independent Methodist Chapel. His son, my grandfather, was the first child to be christened at that chapel. As children, we all went to the Chapel and we were all baptised there.

Stanley

We spent quite a lot of time up at Thornhill Lees Methodist Chapel preparing for concerts, plays and pantomimes. There was a Methodist Chapel on Brewery Lane in the 1840s which was sold to the Kilner Brothers. Mrs Caleb Kilner was presented with a silver trowel at the stone laying ceremony for the new church, built near the junction of Lees Hall Road and Brewery Lane. The doors opened in 1871. A Sunday school was built a few years later and opened by George Kilner. In 1970 a centenary celebration took place, to which members of the Kilner family were invited. Kenneth Kilner attended from America.

Thornhill Lees Parish Church, Holy Innocents

We met at the chapel youth group and we were joint secretaries of the group. We had a religious meeting once a month and a summer fayre once a year. Every year, the choir performed an operetta. This one of The Mikado must have been performed in the 1930s. Fourth from the left on the top row is Mary Watkinson from Watkinson's bakers. Third from the right is George!

Mary & George

Although my three daughters went with their dad to the Sunday service at St Anne's Catholic Church on Lees Hall Road, afterwards they would go to the service at the Primitive Methodist Chapel where they were made especially welcome. There were lots of activities for young people – pantomimes, youth groups and one of the highlights was the Festival of Queens. A girl was chosen to be Queen and two other girls as attendants. Lots of chapels participated and the Festival itself was held at Dewsbury Town Hall and all the proceeds given to the National Children's Homes. When Whitsuntide came around, the Queen would head the procession around the village.

Norma

Queen Rachael is crowned

RACHAEL SWORDS became Thornhill Lees Independent Methodist Church's new Sunday School Queen when she was crowned by Mrs. L. Hathaway at the Mother's Day service.

Rachael, who succeeds Margaret Webster as Queen, has Jane Preston and Simone and Naomi Idle as her attendants.

Sunday School scholars presented a short play with the Mother's Day theme in mind, and prizes were presented to pupils who gained top marks in their section of the

national "Clearway" exam. Tokens were given to those who attained 65 per cent or more.

Top of the section were Nigel Preston, Angela Overend, David Thornton and Margaret Webster. Those with over 65 per cent. were Richard Woodward, Karen Jepson, Karl Jepson and Patricia Randle.

Buttonholes were presented to the children, who in turn presented them to their mothers.

Edgar: one of England's oldest men

In the 1990s, Edgar Sharpe was one of the oldest men in Britain and he lived and worked in Thornhill Lees.

Born in 1886 he attended the school on Slaithwaite Road and he was a choirboy at the local church. He started working at Wormalds & Walker in the engineering shed when he was 13 years old. Edgar always enjoyed dancing, gardening, walking and generally being outside. He was still pottering in his garden at the age of 105. Longevity ran in the Sharpe family. Both his parents lived well into their nineties.

David

They talk about the dirt and pollution of the past but it didn't seem to do Edgar any real harm. There was the railway and goods yard, steam engines running day and night, Ingham's Colliery, the Gas works, Brown's Chemical works, Wormalds & Walker, Kilner's and within another 200 yds, the Savile Town Mills all throwing smoke out and yet England's oldest man lived until he was 108 in Thornhill Lees. People were hardy, their diet was frugal but healthy and they got on with life.

Sidney

Mr Edgar Sharpe, 106 years old. Photo © Dewsbury Reporter

Close to home

In March 1932 my mum became a local celebrity for a while when she and her sister married two brothers.

My mum and aunty lived in Thornhill Lees and my dad and uncle came from Thornhill. They united the two villages in one fell swoop. For a while, the two couples lived in Dale Street with their children and grandparents. My mum and aunty worked for Wormalds & Walker and while my dad was serving in the army during the war, my uncle worked at Radcliffe Mill where they made material for Forces uniforms. The success of working and family life in Thornhill Lees depended on strong family connections and staying close to home and places of work.

Norma

DOUBLE WEDDING AT THORNHILL LEES.

BROTHERS MARRY SISTERS.

MICKLETHWAITE—GREEN.

There was a crowded congregation at the Thornhill Lees Parish Church, on Monday, on the occasion of a double wedding, when two well-known Thornhill Lees sisters married two Thornhill brothers. The Vicar (the Rev. J. E. Roberts) conducted both ceremonies, and in one case contributed organ music as the bride and bridegroom were leaving the church

In the first case, Miss Edith Green, daughter of Mr. and Mrs. Robert Green, of 59, Dale Street, Thornhill Lees, was united to Mr. Harry Micklethwaite, son of Mr. and Mrs. Leonard Micklethwaite, of Caulms Terrace, Thornhill. Miss Green has been a popular teacher at the Parish Church Sunday School, and after the ceremony the vicar played organ music.

In the second case, Miss Annie Green was married to Mr. Frank Micklethwaite.

Given away by their father, the brides looked charming in ankle-length dresses of lace and georgette, with lace coatees. Their wreaths and veils were held in place by orange blossoms, and they carried bouquets of red roses.

The bridesmaids were the same in each case—Misses Nellie Green (cousin of the brides), Alice Micklethwaite (sister of the bridegrooms), Florence Green (cousin of the brides), Elsie Micklethwaite (sister of the bridegrooms), and Dorothy Oade. The two first-named wore blue angel silk, with blue hats, and bouquets of tulips and white narcissi; while the three remaining bridesmaids were also in angel silk, but wore pale blue bonnet-shaped hats and carried similar bouquets.

Mr. Senior Micklethwaite and Mr. Mark Godbold were best men for the respective couples, and Mr. Edmund Senior discharged the duties of groomsman.

A reception in the Working Men's Club was attended by over 70 guests.

Amongst a number of presents was a silver cake basket and a silver cake knife from the teachers of the Parish Church Sunday School.

Newspaper cutting 1932

Edith and Harry (left); Annie and Frank (right)

Village icons

Roy Butcher

Everyone knew Roy in Thornhill Lees. He started as a bus conductor for Yorkshire Woollen Bus Company. Then he progressed to driver and then to one man operator as circumstances changed. He was a lovely bus driver, pleasant, helpful and funny.

He had a habit of leaving things on a low light. He drove his bus back home to Centenary Square once because he'd left his sausages under the grill. He brought the charred remains out to show his passengers. He was a born storyteller.

He was a community-minded man. A family at the top of Thornhill moved to the bottom using his bus; everything that they could lift on to the bus went! Roy played Santa Claus in the bus station. He played Santa for the old folks and the children. He refused to wear the outfit whilst driving buses because it was dangerous!

Left: Roy as conductor   *Above:* Roy as driver

He was chair of the Tenants and Residents' Committee. He was instrumental in organising the children's party once a year on the park before the community centre was built. It was when the Asian community started moving here. He thought if we could get the children together, the adults might follow.

He was on the committee for building the community centre. Sadly he died before it was finished. There were so many people at his funeral from work, TRA, friends etc. - it showed how many people actually knew and respected him.

He was making inroads both before and during the arrival of the South Asian community. Everybody was welcome at his home. 'Anyone can come to my door!' he'd say.

With Roy being a bus driver, everything was to do with keeping time, so I've donated a sundial in his memory on to the Thornhill Lees Senior Citizens' Social Centre (called *Sunshine Corner by Roy*). They've made a little garden at the side as a memory and sensory garden.

Brenda, Roy's wife

Roy with members of the Tenants and Residents Association

Harry and his aeroplanes, remembered by Stuart

Harry Laycock

When we were little there was this man called Harry Laycock. He was a bit like the Pied Piper, taking us children on long walks and he made paper aeroplanes.

He had gone to the Grammar School and been highly educated as far as I believe. His sister lived in the house next door but one to us and she looked after him. He was what you'd call an eccentric but if your child was with Harry, they were safe! He just used to trail about, and kids trailed with him. He was lovely.

Jacqueline

We will always remember going on walks with Harry. We'd go to woods and all the way round Thornhill Lees. Loads of us, definitely over 20 I should say, would follow on and shout 'We're going wi' Harry' and parents were fine with it.

He was very knowledgeable out in the countryside and he made it magical for us. He could've taken us to the ends of the earth and I think we'd have followed him you know, Harry and his amazing planes.

I wish they could have named some of the new buildings or streets around here in remembrance of him because I think we all have good memories of him.

Margaret J

Harry Laycock and his paper aeroplanes

I am writing about a character who we kids in Thornhill Lees thought was awesome. His name was Harry Laycock and he lived in a back to back house close to what was Child's fish shop. Harry was not able to work full time (fortunately for us kids) due to a heart condition which he had been born with. Today this would have been diagnosed by doctors and surgery performed to correct this abnormality. However, he did work part time for one of the local butchers, Harold Leech, and would be seen pedalling along on a delivery bike.

Harry's favourite saying was 'A bonk on the conk' and he would hit you on the top of your head with a rolled up magazine or newspaper. His signature was paper aeroplanes.

Harry Laycock, a true friend of children in Thornhill Lees

If you wanted to find Harry, you just had to follow the trail of paper aeroplanes. These were highly prized by us kids and there was always a mad scramble to get the one that had 'flown the furthest.'

During the school holidays, we would wait expectantly for Harry with our bottles of water and jam sandwiches in a paper bag. He would gather us all together and we would set off in a column along Lees Hall Road. Invariably he would be making his paper planes as he walked along. We'd turn up Green Lane past Sutcliffe's Farm, a quick look in the pond at the top and then under the railway bridge and up Ouzelwell Lane. Then we'd turn right along the footpath and follow the stream past Pepper's farm, and into the wood where we had our rope swing.

Here we would spend some time playing whilst Harry would whittle away on a piece of wood with a penknife. If we were lucky he would point out the natural things of life: rabbit holes, mouse nests, mushrooms and fungi, and in particular the birds' nests. He would carefully take an egg from a nest, and identify it to us before carefully putting it back and telling us that we never had to take eggs from the nest. Then after a short while, we'd jump over the stream and pass Paradise Farm stopping by the pond to look at sticklebacks or frog spawn.

We would finally come to our favourite pond just outside the woods that belonged to the Reformatory. Here, we would paddle, trying to catch the sticklebacks in our hands, but never being successful. If we were lucky we would see the newts. We would sit and eat our sandwiches, basking in the glorious sunshine that in those days seemed to stretch from the first to the last day of the school holidays. Off on our way again, along the footpath and above Ouzelwell farm where 'Three Boys Hill' was located and another one of our favourite spots to play. This area was known by us locals as 'back a

moon' because when the moon was low, it just appeared to be suspended above the cottages that were situated at the top of Ouzelwell Lane.

Sometimes we would meet up with the kids from Thornhill and there would be a challenge to a game of cricket or football. Finally, Harry would call time and we would say our farewells and set off on the last part of our trek home, down back of pit with all the smoke from the coke ovens and the noises associated with the mining industry. Past the weigh bridge and down Pit Lane. Finally, at the bottom, we would say our farewell to Harry and arrive home dirty, tired, but with many a tale to tell our parents.

So there you have a day in my life with Harry. He was a gentle giant. He helped shape our lives and taught us about nature. Our parents had no qualms about us setting off for the day with him for they knew that we would all be well looked after. Unfortunately, today this would probably not happen because society would be treating him with suspicion. How very wrong they would be.

Bill

Trams

The first tram service through Thornhill Lees began in February 1903. The recently formed Yorkshire (Woollen District) Electric Tramway Co. Ltd provided a regular ten minute service between Dewsbury and the terminus at Combs Colliery Thornhill. The route passed through Savile Town and Thornhill Lees.

Work began in 1902 laying tracks and erecting the over head power supply.

The trams on this route had upper decks as there were no low bridges to pass under. They could carry 22 passengers inside and 34 outside (upstairs). Originally the upstairs deck was open topped, but a later modification enclosed it.

Up to the introduction of the tram service, most people would have had to walk to work or town. It must have been a wonderful experience to ride on one for the first time.

The tram service played a vital role in the districts booming economy. They transported thousands of workers daily to and from the mills, mines and factories.

The wages earnt in these prosperous times needed to be spent; the tram once again played its part, taking shoppers to town to the new stores and markets. Money saved was well spent on a tram fare home with heavy bags!

Advertising was allowed on tramcars to provide the operators with extra revenue.

Fares on the trams were about two pennies a mile and half that for children and workers. The tram company also issued plastic tokens for some school children and postmen.

The trams ran for only 30 years. In that time more modern, reliable motor buses became available. These now became the standard form of public transport.

The tram operators changed their name in 1935 to the Yorkshire Woollen District Transport Company Limited.

Trains

Thornhill Lees was fortunate to gain its railway connection eight years before that of Dewsbury. The railway companies had toiled long and hard to connect Dewsbury to the rail network, but the river and the difficult 'Headfield' spur made any sort of access into Dewsbury incredibly difficult. Ultimately, the Lancashire & Yorkshire Railway Company decided on the location of Thornhill Lees for the link to Dewsbury.

In October 1840 the station was opened. Despite being named Thornhill for Dewsbury, it was located in Thornhill Lees. Dewsbury did not gain its own mainline station at Wellington Road until 1848, connecting Leeds and Manchester.

The goods part of the operation transported manufactured items from the Thornhill Lees based industries all over the UK. The massive expanse of goods storage and marshalling yards that ran from Forge Lane through to Thornhill Lees Station made this possible. There were more rails sidings at the side of the canal on Forge Lane and these were continually filled with lines of coal trucks; these rails were connected to the main lines and distributed the coal from the nearby

Ingham's pit in Thornhill. The station closed to passengers in 1962 and ceased goods traffic a year later, although the sidings carried on for some years afterwards.

Stuart

Lees House at the rear of the station was the home of John Walker of Wormalds & Walker and Mayor of Dewsbury in 1889. He opened the new Town Hall in 1889.

We had a chartered train for the Thornhill Lees Club trip. We ran down this ramp on to the platform and we were so excited. They'd give us envelopes with spending money in and we had stewards to look after us. The train went straight to Cleethorpes and didn't stop. We used to meet our cousins there and we'd all get together and just play on the sands.

Margaret

A lot of the industries organised trips for the workers and their families and they all went by train from the station here. Wormalds took a thousand people to the Festival of Britain on several trains. What a treat!

Maurice

First there was an exhibition...

Below left: Visitors at the Transforming Thornhill Lees exhibition

Bottom left: Eileen Fenton with the Mayor of Kirklees, Cllr Julie Stewart-Turner at the exhibition launch in 2009

Below: Nigel and the tram he built for the exhibition

In August 2009, the well known swimmer and former Thornhill Lees resident Eileen Fenton, came to the community centre on Brewery Lane to open the *Transforming Thornhill Lees* exhibition.

Over fifty members of the exhibition group shared treasured objects, photographs and stories which were featured in the displays.

The IT room of the Community Centre was totally transformed. Visitors were delighted by the hardware and chemist shops, the coal wagon, the Kilner's case of bottles, the reproduction tram built by resident Nigel Ingham and the wall mounted *Badges of the Brave* blanket.

Over 400 people attended the launch event and during its stay at the Community Centre, the exhibition was visited by over 2000 people, many of whom travelled from other counties and in some cases other countries!

Subsequently, the exhibition was hosted by Ravenshall School and finally by Dewsbury Museum attracting a further 4,500 people.

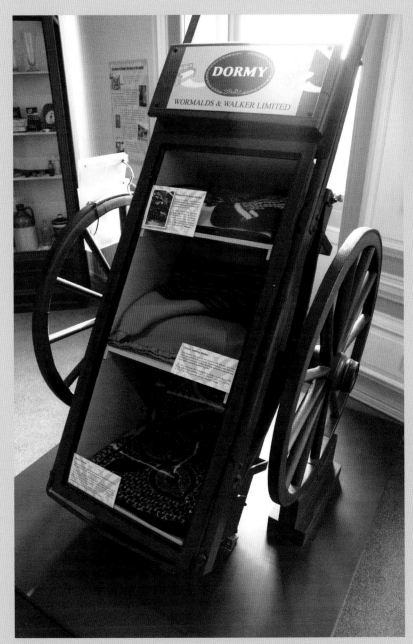

Top: Spitfire blanket

Left: Dormy blanket cart, from the exhibition

Above: Guests at the exhibition launch in 2009

Wiffam Wuffam Band Song

by Andy Burton June 2009
Sung by children from Thornhill Lees
Infant School

Tommy Talkers, Tommy Talkers,
Tommy Talkers, Tommy Talkers

Chorus:

Wiffam Wuffum, Wiffum Wuffum Band
Wiffam Wuffum playing for you
Wiffam Wuffum playing for you

Verse 1

The Mill made blankets for the Queen's bed
Hear the looms rattle in the weaving shed
Rattle, rattle, rattle in the weaving shed
At Ingham's Mine in the dark and dirt
Hear the knock on rock as miners work
Knock, knock, knock as miners work

Eileen swam the channel, first lady ever
Hear the water splash! as her legs kick together
Hear the water splash! as her legs kick together

Chorus:

Wiffam Wuffum, Wiffum Wuffum Band etc

Verse 2

Kilner's made bottles and jars for Jam
Hear the glass chink as they load the van
Chink, chink, chink as they load the van
Coco drove a crane at electric factory
Hear the buzz, buzz of electricity
Buzz, buzz, buzz of electricity

Bus driver Roy, left his oven grill on
Hear bang, bang, bang, sausages gone!
Hear bang, bang, bang, sausages gone!

Chorus:
Wiffam Wuffum, Wiffum Wuffum Band etc

Children from Thornhill Lees Infant school worked with Satellite Arts to recreate the Thornhill Lees Comic Prize Band of 1910.

The band sang a specially written song inspired by stories from the exhibition at the Exhibition Launch event.

The children were thrilled to meet Eileen Fenton!

Top: Thornhill Lees Comic Band 2009

Above: The original band in 1910 (Kirklees Image Archive)

Right: Eileen Fenton with the children

85

If houses could speak...

In 2012, Kirklees Community Heritage team ran a series of local history sessions at Headfield School, supported by members of the exhibition group and writer Gareth Durasow. The young residents of today's Thornhill Lees were asked to think about what the area had been like in the past, what it's like now and how it might be in the future. They were asked to imagine that their homes could speak. What would a house say about the generations of people who lived under its roof? This is what houses in Thornhill Lees would say...

I do not remember if the people who lived here before were nice or not nice, kind or not kind, mean or not so mean. But they made history.

> **I felt lonely a long time ago when the old families left. The decorations were old and the carpets were worn out.**

Left: Corner of Lees Hall Road and Fiddler Hill
(Kirklees Image Archive)

I stand on Park House Drive. I like Aminah because she helps keep me clean and tidy. I think about people who lived in Thornhill Lees before Aminah. They had shops like the one with the carpet sweepers. Carpet sweepers to keep other houses clean without electricity. A long time ago. I look at the patterns on my walls and the flowers outside and look forward to the birthdays.

Aminah

My name is House on Broomer Street. I like Shaamil being active, being funny and scaring his sister with his toy spider. I like him because he listens, he does his homework and he enjoys playing on the outside. I dream of what the family will do tomorrow to make me smile.

Shaamil

I am a house in Thornhill Park. I make it warm and safe for the family to live here. I think of the people who lived here before. I wonder what it feels like to be human here in Dewsbury. I dream of tomorrow when Saiffudin will ride his bike down the hill.

Saiffudin

> **A long time go there were eighteen people living in me. They had no cars. They had to work very hard.**

I am a house on Walker Street. I like that Stanley never stops talking and tells very funny jokes. He keeps James company and makes lots of stuff for his brothers. When he rides his bike down the back ginnel, he sometimes falls off and lands on his bottom. Bang, dash, crash, wheeeeee...

Stanley

My door is on Slaithwaite Road. I have bright bedrooms, a happy living room and a lucky kitchen. I remember when Ruqayah had her parents evening. She came home that day and her mum said "You are a good girl." At night I dream of flowers in my windows, new babies born, the smell of delicious pizza and wedding photos.

Ruqayah

87

I remember the people who lived in me before. They were noisy, they fussed over their clothes, they fought with each other. These people are quiet, they get on and do fun things together.

My name is House on Nursery Grove. I like the people in my rooms because they treat me well. I like Unaysa because she's kind to her family. They always say hello to me when they come back from somewhere. They ask me questions even when I can't answer. I remember the people who lived in me before. They were noisy, they fussed over their clothes, they fought with each other. These people are quiet, they get on and do fun things together.
Unaysa

I am a house on Headfield Road. I like your good behaviour, I like your helpfulness. You look after each other and you keep me clean. Before you moved in, I was lonely.
My old family killed me but now I am a new house, I am alive again. At night I dream of Hafsa's mum having a new baby, a new life. There will be laughing and water fights and happiness.
Hafsa

I am a house on Selbourne Avenue. Hafsah plays with her little sister and little brother outside. They are happy together and try to be kind. I do not remember if the people who lived here before were nice or not nice, kind or not kind, mean or not so mean. But they made history.
Hafsah

My name is House on St Ann's Close. I like the happiness in my rooms and the kind stuff they do. There used to be an old Grandad living here. He used to make bottles for the factory. He worked hard and it was hot. People helped each other. I dream of tomorrow when new things will happen.
Afnan

I am a house on Brewery Lane. I like the people who live in me. They keep me fresh and clean and look after each other. I remember the old miners and glass workers and mill workers who lived on these streets. They walked to work early in the morning and came home to coal fires. I dream about everyone being happy.
Sameer

My name is House on Parker Road. I like the laughter of the children and how they feel safe. There is always nice food cooking in the kitchen. I remember the past and who lived in me then, all the sounds and smells. When I sleep I dream of what the children will do the next morning.
Malyka

My name is house on Scarborough Street. I like Maryam because she is kind and funny. I remember the people who lived here before Maryam. But they were neither kind, nor were they funny. At night I dream of the future when Maryam will leave me forever.
Maryam

My name is House on Douglas Street. I like Mubasharah because she plays with her sisters and brothers. She loves them, cares about them and listens. She helps to keep me clean and is always happy and cheerful. She respects her parents and everyone who visits here. I remember the man who worked in the glass bottle factory. He helped make the bottles that kept the fizz in drinks. I also remember the mill workers who made blankets. And the shop called Cruden's that sold vacuum cleaners that worked without electricity. I dream about all the families who have lived here crying and laughing. Happy occasions, sad moments, parties, babies being born, flowers in the windows. Smiles on all their faces.
Mubasharah

I am a house on Headfield Road. The people I live with are kind and helpful. My garden is neat and the children are well behaved. I felt lonely a long time ago when the old families left. The decorations were old and the carpets were worn out. Now everything is fresh and new. I dream of new days and new things happening.

Halima

My name is House on Pioneer Street. These are my memories: people left me to go to work in the morning, to the mine or the mill and the glass factory. Carrying lanterns, lunch boxes and marbles. Now the people inside me are kind and work hard. I never feel lonely. I dream of a garden with a maze.

Zaid

I am a house on Dale Street. I am clean and bright. I watch cars taking people to places. A long time go there were 18 people living in me. They had no cars. They had to work very hard. I enjoy watching the children playing. The children always play.

Abdurrahman

I am Asif's house. Asif is kind to his brother and he is funny. I remember when my walls were a different colour and there were different voices. At night I dream that Asif has no more school work. He is working hard at something else.

Asif

I am a house in Ashfield. I like the people inside me being happy. Abdullah, you are just the best child ever! I remember who lived here before. A woman and a girl who went to your school before you were born. I dream about everything being perfect inside of me. Sometimes I dream about what you dream.

Abdullah

I am a house on Ingham Road. The family that lives I me is just the best. They make me feel alive. They fill my rooms with the smell of yummy food. I remember the man and woman and child who lived here before. I dream of what might come true in their lives. Dreaming about them is the favourite to me.

Ziyyad

I am a house on Headfield Road. Aaisha and her family keep me neat and tidy and love me. Aaisha plays on her bike outside and does her homework. I'm lucky because I don't have to do homework. I remember the lady that lives on this street. She worked at Wormald & Walkers and her name is Sheila. She made blankets and her father and grandfather made them too. I dream of Aaisha's mum finding a job really quickly. And she is smiling.

Aaisha

I am a house in Hebble Court. I like Safa because she is kind to her sister and listens to her mum. She eats all her food and is good to everybody in her family. I remember the miner who worked in the Thornhill Lees mine. He lived here and burned coal on the fire. I dream of a time when there is no fighting.

Safa

I am a house on Greenwood Street. What I like about Ayesha is her kindness. She is tidy, funny and always respects me. She is also a very crafty girl. I remember the people who used to work in Thornhill Lees making soft and comfy blankets in the mill. Finding coal underground. Making bottles in the factory. I dream about people laughing and having fun. Families playing together and loving each other.

Ayesha

I dream about all the families who have lived here crying and laughing. Happy occasions, sad moments. Parties, babies being born, flowers in the windows. Smiles on all their faces.

Thoughts for the future...

Holding the community together

The landscape of our community has already changed dramatically as a lot of its available spaces have been identified for future housing needs. Thornhill Lees could lose its identity as a village as it becomes just another featureless suburb of Dewsbury with little to offer to its people.

We must ensure that the controversial changes planned for Thornhill lees include improvements that will benefit our present and future community. Our industrious past has left a legacy that could give us an opportunity to create an outstanding asset for everybody to enjoy. We are extremely fortunate to have over a mile of tranquil waterway flowing right through the middle of our community; that's two miles of waterfront with many possibilities to create small recreational areas. Perhaps seats and benches with panels depicting the 'coal, glass, iron and textiles' industries that created Thornhill Lees could provide a lasting link to our wonderful heritage. The community would benefit greatly with more cycle and footpaths and possibly a foot bridge or two over the canal to bring together the fragmented settlements of our village. Perhaps one day Thornhill lees may even get a new canal side park on the site of the old cricket field? It's still there after all these years. The canal transformed our past. Maybe the canal could help transform our future?
Nigel

Sometimes I want to walk all the way to the top of the hill in Thornhill Lees and roll all the way down just because I could and I'm so happy to live in such a green place!
Shazia

Well, the old factory's come down now and there's new housing there so I wonder what it means. What will happen to the balance of the community?
Fatima

New housing might alter things visually, but that alone is not enough. What do you do to create a community again? The two cultures are completely separate and don't have much to do with one another. There's no industry to bind them together. I don't know what you do about that.
Norma

What of the people that live in these two villages, yes I say two, because there is no sign of integration? If there was,

perhaps I could be more positive about the future of the village.
Bill

People have to act to make sure the village is protected. I was involved in the 'Sink the Link' campaign in the early 1990s. There was an idea to build a road to link the M1 and the M62. It would have gone right through the middle of Thornhill Lees. We all went down to London to see Michael Howard, who was transport minister at the time. People who cared did something about it.
David

There are difficult challenges and issues ahead for the village but I believe that diversity is a strength. There is a strength in getting to know one another that enriches culture. The majority of people, regardless of faith, colour or culture all hold the same aspirations for themselves and their children, but they need to share these hopes and dreams.
Khizar

I think Thornhill Lees is doing quite well as long as it stays mixed, then it'll remain a good place to live. As long as our

children grow up and learn to live with other people respecting one another, then Thornhill Lees has a good future.
Kateja

Thornhill Lees has a nice atmosphere and it's still full of good people. I've seen all the industries go but it's a lot cleaner than it used to be. There was a time when you couldn't see the sky so that's some progress.
Maurice

The first year we moved in, it was difficult. We had our windows smashed and people used to say things about us as we went past. After a year it all started to settle down and feel more like home. We got to know our neighbours who helped my mum who was poorly. They were very important people for us.
Yasmin

I love it in Thornhill Lees because you can breathe. I visit people in Savile Town but there it is busy and closed and I can't breathe. I come back here and I say I can't wait to get back to heaven. The people who make decisions should help us to keep this balance.
Shazia

Above: Children on the Church Institute steps

Left: Kateja's mum in the early 1960s with her neighbours

Acknowledgements

This book is dedicated to members of the Exhibition Group who are no longer with us but whose contributions, enthusiasm and love of Thornhill Lees will be long remembered with affection:

Margaret Morris

Mary Coates

Maurice Greenbank

Stanley Oldroyd

George Peace

Kirklees Community Heritage & Education Team and the Transforming Thornhill Lees Exhibition Group would like to thank the following individuals and organisations for their contributions to this book:

Keith Allatt
Bill Beattie
Malcolm Blackburn
Patricia Brookes
Sidney Brooke
Brenda Butcher
Marlene Chambers
Mary Coates
Christine Croisdale
Jacqueline and Roy Ellis
Keith Gibson
Maurice and Barbara Greenbank
Paul Hadley
Edna Haggel
Margaret Hall
Joan Haley
Stuart Hartley
Stanley Hodge
Helen Holdsworth
David Horsman
Shazia Hussain
Yasmin Hussain
Nigel Ingham
Khizar Iqbal
Margaret Jennings
Fatima Lakhi
Frank Long
Jeffrey, Sheila and Susan Lynn
Rex Mellor
Margaret Morris
Richard Morris

Ronald Myers
George and Mary Peace
Stanley Oldroyd
Thelma Pagett
Jean Preston
Dorothy Ramsden
Mike and Shirley Ann Roberts
Kateja Saiyed
Trevor Senior
Gillian Shaw
Norma Swords
Leslie Walker
Muriel Wilkinson
Pat Wilkinson

For extra images and photographs:

Kirklees Image Archive
Photographer Amanda Crowther for cover image
Stuart Hartley
John Flowers
John F Goodchild
Margaret Watson and The Dewsbury Reporter
Malcolm East
Joan Rodwell
Norman Ellis
Pen & Sword Books
Susan Day & Michael Piper (www.glassby.com)
Standard Patent Glazing
Derek Bedford, Dewsbury Mills